More Memories of Bradford

Volume II

Part of the
Memories
series

More Memories of **BRADFORD II**

The Publishers would like to thank the following companies for supporting the production of this book

Main Sponsor
Hart & Clough

WR & R Atkinson Limited

Bombay Stores

Bradford & Ilkley Community College

Buckles

Congregational & General Insurance plc

Joseph Dawson

The Drum Engineering Company Limited

Drummond Group plc

Joseph A Hey & Son Limited

Arnold Laver (Bradford) Limited

Mansfield Pollard & Company Limited

Polestar Watmoughs Limited

HC Slingsby plc

J Wood & Sons Limited

Woolcombers

First published in Great Britain by True North Books Limited
England HX3 6AE
Tel. 01422 377977

© Copyright: True North Books Limited 1999
This edition reprinted in paperback, 2002

All rights reserved. No part of this publication may be reproduced, stored in a retrieval system, or transmitted in any form, or by any means, electronic, mechanical, photocopy, recording or otherwise without the prior permission in writing of the Copyright holders, nor be otherwise circulated in any form or binding or cover other than in which it is published and without a similar condition being imposed on the subsequent publisher.

ISBN 1 903204 65 8

More Memories of **BRADFORD II**

Memories are made of this

© Walter Scott (Bradford) Ltd

Memories. We all have them; some good, some bad, but our memories of the city we grew up in are usually tucked away in a very special place in our minds. The best are often connected with our childhood and youth, when we longed to be grown up and paid no attention to adults who told us that these were the best years of our lives. We look back now and realise that they were right.

So many memories of the Bradford we once knew: smoke rising from every mill chimney, riding on trolley buses, our first pint at The Bod, shopping at Busbys, driving Jowett cars, seeing films at the Ritz and the Theatre Royal. And so many changes! The sweeping away of buildings such as the Swan Arcade, the Prince's Theatre, Kirkgate Market, the Mechanics Institute, the Exchange Station...and the emergence of a new city centre with the Arndale Centre, the Interchange, Centenary Square - and as a bonus, the magic of Imax films and the Photography Museum.

The city has had its bad times along with the good, but through them all Bradford rolled up its sleeves, survived the lean years, and in the end prospered. We have only to compare our present city, with its exciting developments in sport and leisure, commerce and the arts, with Bradford as it was, say in the 1940s, to see what progress has been realised and what achievements have been made over the last 50 years. Bradford has a history we can all be proud of - and just as importantly, a great future to look forward to, into the new millennium and beyond.

More Memories of **BRADFORD II**

Contents

Section one
The streets of change

•

Section two
High days and holidays

•

Section three
A sporting life

•

Section four
Bird's eye view

•

Section five
Down at the shops

•

Section six
Fares, please!

•

Section seven
Outskirts

•

Section eight
Earning a crust

More Memories of **BRADFORD II**

The streets of change

Standing in the middle of Westgate for a 'cal' is not to be recommended today, though in the late 1920s these two men chatting near the lamp standard were no doubt safe enough. Few Bradfordians will remember Milletts being situated on this corner, which is more likely to be associated with Lingards in the minds of a later generation. This photograph shows that at the time Lingards occupied premises on the opposite side of Westgate. A large sign outside Milletts reminds passers-by that they are the 'famous government contractors'; their surplus goods would have been sold at cheaper prices than the average high street outfitters charged; note the range of jackets hanging outside the shop door. The street is busy with shoppers, who, you will notice, are all wearing hats. The headgear is assorted, with a bowler, a trilby and several flat caps amongst the men, while the women obviously preferred the cloche that was all the rage at the time. Whatever the style of hat, few would have ventured out bareheaded whether it was winter or summer; old and young alike felt undressed without their hat.

> *Few people today would be brave enough to stand in the middle of Westgate for a 'cal'*

More Memories of BRADFORD II

Above: You could say that this view along Kirkgate is broadly similar today. The cars have changed, though they now travel in the opposite direction, and the names above the shops have changed; the biggest change of all is of course the Arndale Centre. The building that at the time of the photograph was Novello's was part of the Kirkgate building, bulldozed in 1973. The Old Peculier, whose 'peculier' spelling raised a number of eyebrows when it was first opened, now slakes the thirst of Bradfordians in the same spot, and has become a very popular city centre pub. The Arndale itself, when the dust of the Kirkgate Market controversy had settled, began to worm its way into our affections, and today is so much a part of the life of the city that we couldn't imagine being without it. It has so much to offer us: the indoor market where dozens of stalls offer thousands of goodies, from confectionery to cosmetics; the large stores such as Boots, W H Smith and Littlewoods, and the smaller shops offering shoes, fashions, stationery, jewellery, health foods and china. And when the shopping is done we can relax in the open refreshment area with a mug of coffee, just watching the world go by.

The Old Peculier now stands where Novello's once was

6

More Memories of BRADFORD II

Below: Through all the changing scenes of life...people need to go shopping. We can see that Westgate has much to offer shoppers, with Lingards department store on the right and a selection of smaller shops on the left. A bargain might have been had at the time, as Heys, on the corner of Godwin Street (thought to sell menswear), are holding a sale; the adjoining business is an optician - which it still is today. Growing traffic levels down Westgate in recent years called for a pelican crossing to be introduced where the motor cycle and sidecar is parked in this busy scene. A number of old advertisements add interest to the view: Swan Vestas matches, Wills Gold Flake cigarettes and Bovril. Early Bovril slogans were not without a touch of humour ('I hear they want more!' says one nervous bull to another), and their ingenuity made Bovril into a household name. Interestingly, the catch-phrase 'Bovril prevents that sinking feeling' was designed before World War I but was withheld at the time as a mark of respect for the families of those lost on the 'Titanic' in 1912.

Bottom: What a wonderful old photograph! The atmosphere of the old city centre is recaptured in this view taken at the junction of Market Street and Cheapside. Gas lamps still formed much of the city's street lighting, and this junction, lit by four arc lamps on a beautifully designed pillar, would have been brilliantly lit in comparison. The road numbers are very clearly marked on these road signs; it was 1919 when British roads were numbered. Strangers driving to Harrogate, however, would have been left scratching their heads in bewilderment at being given a choice of three routes that went in three totally different directions!

Note the rather nice umbrella shop on the corner on the right; the umbrella mounted outside leaves passers-by in no doubt about the goods on sale there, though we can't quite read the name above the window. These buildings and many of those on the left, including the Swan Arcade, were demolished in 1964 as part of the city's redevelopment scheme.

More Memories of BRADFORD II

It is difficult to visualise, as we stand in Centenary Square, the towering bulk of the impressive buildings that once occupied the empty space. These included the Mechanics Institute, to the left of the photograph, where posters advertising forthcoming events just creep into the picture. It would be interesting to be able to read them and find out exactly what concerts and meetings were on the programme for that particular week! The shop facing us on the corner of Tyrrel Street and Sunbridge Road was at that time selling poultry and game, and we can see from the number of birds

More Memories of BRADFORD II

hanging on view in the window that a chicken dinner was as popular then as it is now. During the 1920s and 30s, of course, it was likely to have been served with sage and onion stuffing, roast potatoes and vegetables, whereas a good number of today's chicken lovers would probably choose to eat it in a good Bradford curry! Interestingly, this photograph reveals that the Saxone shoe shop was at that time on the corner of Tyrrel Street, though perhaps readers will more readily remember the shop on the other side of the Mechanics Institute, on the corner of Market Street.

More Memories of BRADFORD II

Above: Bradford's most famous landmark - the 220 ft high clock tower that dominated the skyline in the days before high-rise buildings - still takes pride of place in the city. Lovers of detail will enjoy reading that the largest bell in the clock tower is named Big Matthew William in honour of the Mayor, Alderman Matthew Thompson, who performed the opening ceremony in 1873. Workers were given a holiday, and an enormous crowd of people flooded the city centre. The new building cost around £100,000 - a snip at today's prices, but a large amount of money at that time. Thirty-five beautifully-sculpted statues of kings and queens of England were mounted in niches around the building; spot some of them at second-floor level in this photograph. The earliest king portrayed was William the Conqueror, who invaded our shores in 1066, and the latest was, of course, Queen Victoria. Interestingly, Oliver Cromwell, who was offered the crown but refused it, gained a niche on Bradford Town Hall.

Right: Seen from second-floor level this marvellous photograph makes these lofty buildings in Tyrrel Street and Ivegate look even taller and more impressive. It's many years since we had to dodge traffic in Ivegate, and a decade or more since we could pop into the Unicorn for a pint of Tetleys. Narrow, steep and busy, this favourite street has over the years supplied a wide range of goods to Bradfordians. Food, music, clothes, shoes, jewellery and decorating materials; it was all there in this one street. A number of readers will remember their school days when they got kitted out in the uniforms of Bolling and Carlton Grammar and all the other Bradford upper schools at Tose and Smiths. Our fathers could shop at Dunns gents' outfitters on the corner of Hustlergate at the bottom of the hill (now a cafe bar) while our mothers joined the long queue outside Philip Smith's pork butchers, whose succulent pork pies were legendary. And remember Freeman Hardy & Willis? Just one of a number of shoe shops in Ivegate. Liquid refreshment was not left out, with the Unicorn, Yates's Wine Lodge, the Grosvenor, later a Berni Inn then the Ram's Revenge and today Fates & Firkin, and, of course, The Old Crown.

More Memories of BRADFORD II

Below: Centenary Square was undreamed of when this view was captured for posterity sometime during the 1940s. The branch of Saxone shoes on the left was familiar to Bradfordians for many years; note that the reading rooms of the adjoining Mechanics Institute were situated above the shoe shop. This Victorian building fell victim to the bulldozer in the early 1970s, and in recent years Centenary Square was laid out here with more aesthetic taste than was shown in the earlier changes of the 60s and 70s.

The square is appreciated by most Bradfordians today, and often sees lively action from local bands to the odd funfair. Important to the city is the memorial to those who perished in the Valley Parade fire in 1985. The background view remains much the same today, as the bottom of Sunbridge Road was left alone by the developers. Alfred Waterhouse's beautiful pink granite and red brick Prudential building, with its elegantly styled windows and pediments, is well worth a second look. The building is today occupied by the Co-operative Bank.

Right: Sunbridge Road was not so different in 1946 than it is today, with one exception that Bradfordians will instantly spot. The Empress pub today occupies the position of the block of buildings below Queen Anne Chambers, a spot conveniently marked for us by a narrow gap in the shadow thrown on the road. Here, a well-worn stone stairway descends to Aldermanbury. Sunwin House, which can be seen in the distance in Godwin Street, looks little different today and remains a well-known and popular store. Though it has never been a major shopping street, Sunbridge Road has always had its retail premises. The ground floor of the Refuge Building on the bottom corner of Sunbridge Road has long been occupied by shops, and today a fish and chip restaurant, charity shop and a pizza takeaway are in residence there, with Alldays small supermarket next door above. Readers will remember Woods Music Shop on the right, which in recent years relocated to larger premises on Manningham Lane, and Lingards department store on the top corner. Their previous premises were not too far away at the corner of Westgate and Godwin Street - one of the few premises to suffer from Nazi bombs during World War II.

© Walter Scott (Bradford) Ltd

More Memories of BRADFORD II

Above: The camera records that the sparkling revue 'London, Paris, Berlin' was playing at the Alhambra when this scene was snapped in 1929. The Alhambra we know and love, but the railings on the right of the photograph will perhaps be unfamiliar to younger readers. This marked the boundary of the old Horton Lane Congregational Church which was demolished forty years or so ago. The chapel may be gone but the Sunday School remains as Glyde House, nearby in Little Horton Lane. A couple of trams, once a familiar sight in their smart navy and cream livery, can be seen at the bottom of Morley Street (where they cut right through the centre of Victoria Square roundabout!). Numbers 1, 2 and 3 carried passengers into town by way of Morley Street from Wibsey, Horton Bank Top and Queensbury - and the return journey usually included two or three bikes belonging to people who had cycled into town and caught the bus back! This part of Bradford had many retail shops at the time as well as a number of theatres and a cinema, and the whole area buzzed with life. In Little Horton Lane the Princes' Theatre and the Palace Theatre kept people entertained with plays and music hall.

Above right: The Boars Head was demolished in the early 1960s, but in its day it served Bradford well, with food as well as with the odd pint of locally-brewed White Rose. Below ground level in Market Street was the popular Bodega Bar, its nickname 'The Bod' officially shortened and displayed in the window. At the time this photograph was taken, the late 1940s or early 50s at a guess, the old building was looking distinctly run down. It was nevertheless a splendid building; strip off its outer layer of soot and the Boars Head would have come to life. Those carved heads at first-floor level for example - no less than 13 of them in this fascinating picture - would immediately command attention. There must be a story attached to these effigies that had been rendered almost invisible by decades of smoke; who were they, and why were they carved on this old inn? We will probably never know, but they lend their own touch of mystery to the Boars Head's sturdy elegance.

More Memories of BRADFORD II

Below: Those were the days! Pedestrianised areas were unheard of and not needed in the 1940s when Town Hall Square traffic numbered two cars and a couple of trams. The Town Hall is now the City Hall, and Town Hall Street, where the trams are waiting, has now been renamed Channing Way, but readers who have only ever known the modernised city centre will still recognise this view.

The photograph shows the extension that was added to the original 70ft high Town Hall in 1909. You can see 'the join' but by and large the addition blends well with the older building on the left. The old Town Hall's foundation stone was laid on 10th August 1870, and interestingly a time capsule containing various artefacts was placed in the foundations. That would be fascinating to see, but we must hope that it will be many long years before this wonderful building is demolished and people yet unborn are able to see what's inside the time capsule.

Bottom: Town Hall Square roundabout with hardly any traffic - an unusual sight even when this photograph was taken! Totally unrecognisable today, this view contrasts the angular architecture of the Central garage, Bradford's main Austin showroom, with the ecclesiastical lines of the Unitarian church and Channing Hall. The bottom of Manchester Road, with its customary white coated police officer on point duty, is further along, with Morley Street in the distance. The dome is that of the Gaumont, today the Odeon cinema. Readers may well have quaffed the odd pint or three of John Smiths at the New Inn, which stood for well over a hundred years on the corner of Thornton Road. In its early years the New Inn must have been an even livelier place than the one we remember; it was once well known for its stabling facilities - and for its pig market. Around the same time the inn was a venue for Bradford's magistrates' court. Not, it is hoped, on pig market day.

More Memories of **BRADFORD II**

Above: The stony gaze of W E Forster, the great pioneer of education, surveys the changes made in the square that was given his name; at least he would have recognised the Wool Exchange, the lovely old building with the clock tower, top right. The open space between Market Street and Broadway at the top right of the photograph awaits the building of the modern blocks that would become familiar to us as Boots the Chemist's department store (now Mothercare), H Samuel the jewellers, and other shops. The subway is here in the process of construction right outside the door of British Home Stores. Petergate, today a main thoroughfare, is yet to be created, though a group of warehouses in Well Street have been flattened to make room for the new road, and sections of sewer pipe await fitting. Petergate has over the years possessed a number of shops; remember the Fine Fare supermarket? It never realised its potential as a popular shopping street, however, and is today a rather depressed area with a number of vacant properties.

Right: Forster Square in the 1950s, and this spot between the ends of Canal Road and Bolton Road is almost unrecognisable when compared with the same place today. The vehicles in the centre traffic lane are heading around the roundabout, past the main Post Office, and are likely to be turning left up Church Bank. The lorry on the left is about to turn into Bolton Road, a manoeuvre which is no longer possible on today's widened road system. This area saw many changes during the 'clean sweep' of the 60s and 70s. The Post Office closed and a new one was built near Forster Square station; new buildings and a new entrance were added in front of the station; new stores such as Boots (which later became Mothercare), British Home Stores and the Fine Fare supermarket, were built. Warehouses in Well Street were demolished to create Petergate, which carries the traffic from Forster Square towards Leeds Road and Hall Ings. Nearby Little Germany fared better, and conservation schemes have preserved the historic buildings there. The low-level shops on the left of the photograph replaced a burnt-out warehouse, but only temporarily. They too were demolished.

More Memories of BRADFORD II

This dramatic aerial photograph shows the extent of the damage caused by fire that destroyed a warehouse at the junction of Canal Road and Bolton Road in the 1950s. In Canal Road a fire engine is still at the scene, and groups of people, attracted by the drama, have gathered near the old Post Office. Readers may remember the row of single-storey shops that eventually replaced the burnt-out warehouse; you could buy a wide range of goods there, from typewriters to plants and flowers.

Their situation well away from the main city centre stores meant that these little shops became an important port of call for hungry workers from nearby offices. This row of shops had a short life span, and were themselves demolished when Forster Square was redesigned and rebuilt.

The office block to the rear of this warehouse was largely occupied by Grattan Warehouses, the Bradford Catalogue that was big at the time and has become enormous since.

More Memories of BRADFORD II

Not a double yellow line in sight, and traffic was sparse when this photograph was taken in the 1950s. Virtually the only car circuiting the roundabout is a rather nice old Vauxhall Velox; contrast this view with today, when a constant flow of vehicles chokes the city (though not this exact spot, thanks to Princes Way and Hall Ings). The Tyrls is roughly where the roundabout used to be. Keen-eyed readers will perhaps spot the four-legged transport trotting along Market Street, bringing to mind those gentler days when noise from the town's vehicles involved only the rattle of wheels and the clopping of hooves, and the only traffic pollution could be put to good use on the land!

The much loved Farmer Giles' Milk Bar was nearby in Tyrrel Street; it disappeared along with Collinson's Cafe next door. Most of the fine old buildings in Tyrrel Street and Market Street, beyond Town Hall Square, were demolished in Bradford's fashionable rush for redevelopment in the 1960s and 70s.

More Memories of BRADFORD II

Below: Trolley bus Number 794, here seen plying the Number 46 Buttershaw route along Tyrrel Street, began life in St Helens, Lancashire, in 1951 and was acquired along with seven others from the town by Bradford Corporation Transport in 1958. Buying second-hand vehicles was standard procedure, and over the years Bradford had acquired buses from towns and cities around the UK including Swansea, Maidstone, Darlington, Brighton and London; in 1953 Bradford took over the entire fleet of trolley buses from the Notts & Derbys Traction Company when they converted to motor buses. Number 794 served Bradford well before it was scrapped in 1968.

The back of the Mechanics Institute can be seen on the right; the Mechanics was a popular venue for meetings of all kinds before it was demolished in 1974. The empty space it left became Centenary Square in recent years. In the distance readers will be able to pick out the popular Brown Muffs store, a little more upmarket than some other city centre stores. Do you remember the two lifts whose polite attendants would take you to the department you wanted? They don't have service like that any more!

Bottom: This pigeon's eye view takes us back to a Forster Square poised on the threshold of sweeping change. Many of the old familiar buildings have already been demolished, and new constructions along Broadway are in the process of completion. The sites for the L-shaped block of new buildings that would be constructed in front of the station, and for the new main Post Office, have yet to be cleared.

A few readers might remember the short lived but well patronised single-storey row of shops that faced Forster Square. The shops were constructed partly on the site that had housed a warehouse which had been destroyed by fire and later demolished. Only a few years on the shops were themselves demolished as part of the Forster Square redevelopment. The solid though soot-encrusted building on the right of the photograph is the old Post Office (recently sold - watch this space); Bradford Cathedral is tucked away behind where nobody can see it. What planner of old do we have to thank for this piece of daftness?

More Memories of BRADFORD II

Bottom: A photograph to bring back many memories to Bradfordians who remember shopping in Lingards, a department store that is gone but not forgotten. Situated on the corner of Godwin Street and Westgate, Lingards was not among the largest stores in town but it was well liked by shoppers. The menswear shop (today Greenwoods), directly opposite Lingards on the corner of Westgate, has long been a favourite with the well-dressed Bradford man. Halfords, who at one time concentrated more on cycles and accessories than on motoring, occupied the premises next door to Lingards before they moved out to their large store in Manningham Lane. The new store is not only conveniently placed near the town centre but it offers customers ample parking - an important plus factor for a shop selling motoring accessories. Adjacent to Halfords in this picture is Mario and Mary's fashionable and well-patronised hairdressing salon.

It takes a photograph such as this one, that shows a Duckworth Lane trolley bus travelling up Godwin Street, to remind us that not too many years ago traffic ran in both directions. Today, of course, vehicles go down this part of Godwin Street but never up it.

Right: Amazing, isn't it, that cars and lorries always seem to break down in the worst possible places? Give a car a length of road and the engine will cough its last on the roundabout at the end of it. This embarrassing situation has developed on the Town Hall Square roundabout, where a broken down lorry belonging to Bell's Transport Services is causing the driver of this Number 37 trolley bus a few headaches. The driver has to get his bus around the lorry and negotiate the roundabout before he can get to the Clayton stop in Thornton Road, and guided by an inspector he gingerly edges his bus to the full extent of its trolley booms. And what's the betting that behind this little lot the traffic is stacked up all along Thornton Road and Manchester Road? A situation to make any driver want to dig a hole and jump into it.

On a different note, a sharp eyed reader will spot cranes and scaffolding around the Provincial building - now the Abbey National - which is being constructed in the background. On the right, the prices charged by Ridings electricals are worth a mention; a down payment of two shillings (ten pence) in the pound would secure any electrical goods you wanted.

More Memories of **BRADFORD II**

Above: A view to prompt a few memories among readers who had forgotten that John Street had ever looked like this! These properties were nearing the end of their allotted time, however, and a few of the shops on the top side of John Street have already been boarded up prior to demolition. The redevelopment swept away not only the buildings opposite the Rawson Hotel but John Street open market to the rear of the properties. The covered-in market building that replaced it offered less draughty conditions plus an excellent selection of modern shops, a bank, Morrison's supermarket and a roomy car park. In time the John Street shopping facility was accepted and became well-liked by Bradford shoppers. The trolley wires in the photograph are rather puzzling, as John Street did not form part of any trolley bus route. Similarly, tram lines once ran along John Street, but these were only used when a match was playing at Valley Parade; perhaps the trolley bus wires were there for the same reason?

Top: Those who spent the odd penny at the toilets on the roundabout in Town Hall Square (embarassingly situated - everybody knew where you were going!) will remember the general cleanliness of the establishment that is to be envied today, when public funds rarely run to a full-time employee. This facility boasted an attendant who, armed with a cleaning cloth, would enter every cubicle before you to check on the condition of the loo and its seat. Brownie points for Bradford's 'Crystal Palace'! Those were the 'good old days' when a glass roof was free from the unwanted attention of vandals.
And remember The Yorkshire when its name had the word 'penny' in it? The Yorkshire Penny Bank and the Keighley and Craven Building Society in the right foreground were swept away with the rest of the buildings at the bottom of Manchester Road, and today the central police headquarters occupy a good deal of the site in the new stretch of road known as Princes Way.

More Memories of **BRADFORD II**

High days and holidays

Above: Boating on Wibsey Park lake on a Sunday afternoon is one of those pleasant pastimes that in the second half of the 20th century somehow got left behind. In those more gentle days of simple pleasures, all the city's boating lakes were a hive of activity; not only fathers with children but couples and friends would hire a boat and take a turn or two around the island. And if you were enjoying yourself it was easy to feign deafness when the call came: 'Come in Number Ten'! On sunny days the local park was a magnet for scores of people, and those who didn't care for boating could stroll among the flower beds chatting with a friend, or sit by the paddling pool to watch the children enjoying themselves in the water.

Parks have been providing Bradford with open space and fresh air for more than 100 years - a commodity that was desperately needed in the squalid, overcrowded, smoke-plagued conditions of 1850, when Peel Park, the first of Bradford's 32 parks, was opened.

Right: A visit to Myrtle Park in Bingley was as good as a trip to Blackpool back in 1928, as this spot had all the ingredients that make for enjoyment: rocks to climb on, earth and mud (it hardly deserves the label of 'sand') to dig in, and lots of water for wading, paddling - and splashing your sister in the face. A fine sunny day was the added bonus, and these children are making the very best of what would have been a wonderful day out. A picnic basket promises a teatime treat for one young family, whose spades lie ready for action on the rocks; the tough pastime of digging was obviously the 'in thing' among the boys.

This part of the River Aire by the island, seen in the background, was later railed off and a paddling pool provided for the children. Paddling pools were fun, of course, but not a patch on the excitement and adventure that this magic spot provided. The pool has now been filled in, however, today's children sadly preferring the sophistication of their computers to the simple pleasures of paddling. Myrtle Park, however, goes on bringing pleasure to local people visiting the annual Bingley Show, pop concerts, jazz weekends and regular band concerts.

Bottom: What could be nicer than a Sunday afternoon walk in Lister Park? In the days before the family car was looked on as a necessity, the simple pleasures that Bradford's most popular park had to offer were taken up, not only by the local residents but by couples and families all over the city.

Lister Park started life as the estate of Samuel Cunliffe Lister. Bradford Corporation bought the estate in 1870 for £40,000, which sounds a snip to anyone judging by today's prices; back then it was a very large sum of money! Unemployment was a problem even in the late 19th century, and nine years after the park opened, unemployed men were given a job building Lister Park lake. Lister's mansion house was demolished and Cartwright Hall was built on the site; the art gallery and museum was opened in a blaze of glory by the Prince and Princess of Wales in 1904. An inaugural exhibition was held between May and October, with bands playing every day, a crystal maze, a display of goods made in Bradford, and even a Somali village.

Right: A blast from the past for those who remember Northcliffe Gardens as they used to be. The beautifully laid-out and well-manicured park has long been a haven of peace for the people of Shipley, and many hearts must have sunk when these allotments on the right were replaced by blocks of flats. But the parkland today is even more beautiful than it was then, and the area of grassland where these children sat in the spring sunshine has since been very naturally landscaped with trees, bushes and rocks. The hedged semicircle is still there (though sadly the seats are not), and nearby a gateway divides the gardens from the car park that replaced these flower beds of old. The passage of time has turned a pleasant garden walk into a popular beauty spot.

As we look across the valley towards Wrose we can see that new estates of houses are already beginning to fill up the green fields, with Prospect Mount climbing the hill towards Carr Lane. We can trace Carr Lane itself as it mounts the hillside, and on the right, Gaisby Lane and Bolton Woods Quarry. Virtually the only changes to the shops along the main road are in the names above the doors.

More Memories of **BRADFORD II**

Above: The weather had to be very warm before you were brave enough to go swimming at the Lido, but there were always some intrepid souls who would defy the British weather to don their swimming costumes at Bradford's only outdoor pool. These scenes were captured in 1939, and though the day looks quite pleasant there are still more people sitting around the water than swimming in it! The style of swimwear has changed more than a little since then; a few of the men are still sporting all-in-one costumes with shoulder-straps, and although the odd two-piece costume can be seen among the ladies, bikinis were undreamed of back then. It was 1946 when the skimpy costumes were created by French designer Louis Réard, and the daring new swimwear that revealed flesh hitherto unseen in public was immediately labelled indecent and immodest....If they could see us now! Swimming caps (usually made of white rubber and with an uncomfortable strap that fastened under the chin), were customary among the ladies, and remained popular until recent years. Today, their use seems to have all but been abandoned - probably because they never did keep out the water anyway! Was it during the 1960s that coloured flowers (rubber of course!) were added to brighten up the ugly caps?

Bradford Lido was opened in 1930 and remained a popular summer outing for many years. In the end, however, an estimated £60,000 was needed for urgent repairs. The Council decided not to go ahead, and in 1973 they closed the pool. Eventually glue sniffers, vandals and the homeless moved in and in 1991 the Lido was demolished.

More Memories of BRADFORD II

Remember 3D, and those cardboard red-and-green spectacles? Three-dimension viewing was a fad that caught on during the 1950s. 'Kiss Me Kate', playing at the Ritz when this photograph was taken, was shown in 3D, and its realistic effect made Kathryn Grayson and Howard Keel come alive. The magnificent Ritz cinema on Broadway opened on 8 May 1939 to the sound of Joseph Seal playing the cinema's magnificent three-manual organ. The growing popularity of television in the 1950s led to the slow decline of cinemagoing, not only in Bradford but countrywide. The Ritz, however, remained popular long after many local 'flea pits' had gone 'eyes down' to Bingo or closed their doors for ever. But the knell of doom had sounded, and even developing the Ritz into a triple screen cinema in 1974 gave the management no more than a temporary respite from the reality of declining audiences. You may remember seeing one of the last films to be shown - 'Rita, Sue and Bob Too'. The cinema closed down in 1985.

The growing popularity of television in the 1950s led to the slow decline of cinemagoing

More Memories of BRADFORD II

Below: The Empire Theatre was originally the Empire Music Hall, and was built in 1899 at the rear of the Alexandra Hotel, at that time itself only 20 years old. Access to the music hall was through the hotel; note the large sign 'Step This Way' under the canopy. The sign was illuminated by electric light bulbs after dark, as was the 'Empire' sign atop the building; brilliant and attractive it must have been in a city still lit by gas lamps. At sixpence a seat the pit was obviously *The* place to sit, while less well-off punters could sit in the gallery for fourpence. If you were down on your luck, the sum of threepence would buy you a seat way up in 'the gods'. In 1972 the Alexandra Hotel became part of Bradford and Ilkley Community College, but over the years the building deteriorated, and by 1987 only the basement and the ground floor were safe to use. The building was demolished in 1994 and the site became a car park.

Bottom: The Bronte sisters had brought recognition to Haworth as long ago as the late 1920s, when this fascinating view of the famous main street was captured. Bradfordians can, of course, be proud of the fact that Charlotte, Branwell, Emily and Anne Bronte were all born in Market Street, Thornton.
Visitors to Haworth, like this group of well-dressed ladies, were already beginning to make their presence felt as they wandered around the church and the old graveyard, and viewed the Parsonage where the Bronte family lived. More intrepid souls would tramp the hills in search of the 'real' Wuthering Heights or gaze at the stone bridge on the moors where the feet of the gifted but sadly short-lived sisters once trod. Today, of course, consumerism goes hand in hand with the famous Bronte name, and this same simple street is now awash with tearooms, antique shops and gift shops. A little of the old flavour remains with the apothecary, just out of sight on the right, which once supplied Branwell, the Bronte family's black sheep, with his opium. Though opium is not now on offer, you can still buy bars of Sunlight soap for your kitchen floor, blocks of Snowfire for your chilblains, and tapers to light your fire.

More Memories of BRADFORD II

Bottom: Everyone loves a parade, and huge crowds have turned out to see this procession of commercial vehicles in Manningham Lane. We cannot be sure of the date of this photograph, but the rather modern look of the parade is belied by the fact that it certainly took place during the days of the Corporation Gas Department, which was nationalised in 1948. In the days when television sets were a rare luxury confined to the more affluent Bradfordian, events such as this were well-attended. The children might not have been very thrilled to see vehicles such as the Bradford Cleansing Department 'dustcart', which they could see for nothing up their own street every Wednesday morning, but their parents would have been interested in viewing the Gas Department's up-to-the-minute kitchen appliances, and the fine display of engineering exhibits from Crofts. Thornton Engineering, on the right, were a large motor vehicle suppliers, specialising in Hillman, Humber, Sunbeam, Singer, Standard and Triumph cars.

Right: In its heyday Busbys attracted a large number of well-to-do customers, and we can see by the sheer number of manicurists employed at the store that there was no shortage of ladies who could afford the luxury of professional attention to their nails and cuticles.

Treatment at the Manicure Bar cost one shilling - five new pence in today's currency, if not in value. A shilling went a long, long way back in the 1940s, but in terms of personal satisfaction and well-being the filing, buffing and polishing seems cheap at the price.

Manicure was only one of the beauty treatments available to ladies at Busbys. In the days before conditioner and Loving Care were on every supermarket shelf, the hairdressing department included dyeing and reconditioning on their list of services. Can you believe that back then a perm cost around £1? Gentlemen were not forgotten; while they were waiting for their wives they could pop along to Busby's barber's shop for a short back and sides.

More Memories of BRADFORD II

Above: For many years after its change of name in 1950, Bradfordians still went on calling the Gaumont cinema the 'New Vic'. The New Victoria was built in the late 1920s, tempting Bradford cinemagoers with a cafe and a ballroom as well as a cinema; its stylish interior with plush sofas, ornate ceilings and tiled floors made it seem more like a top-class hotel. In its heyday the cinema could seat a staggering 3,300 people. As we know, the Gaumont was to become the Odeon Twin Cinema; the old ballroom was later converted into the Odeon 3. The Alhambra theatre is a very special place to all Bradfordians, a mixture of Charlie Chester, 'Swan Lake', 'Cats' and 'Whistle Down the Wind' weaving themselves into our memories across the years. Remember the pantomimes we saw there as children? Interactive or what! Boos and hisses. Cinderella and Buttons; the fairy godmother; the ugly sisters and, of course, the prince, complete with shapely legs and high heels. The times we shouted 'He's behind you!' and responded to the inevitable 'Oh no he isn't' with 'Oh yes he is!' Great stuff.

Below: This marvellous old photograph captures the energy and excitement of cinema in the days when 'talkies' were the latest thing. 'Book seats now for Saturday!' booms a huge sign on the side wall of the Theatre Royal. Those who did so would obviously have been in for a treat, as the 'all talking' film 'Young Woodley' was being screened - a film, we learn from the many notices posted around the building, that had been adapted from the 'sensational West-End Play'. Under the canopy, stills from the movie attract passers-by, and there were many of them, the cinema being situated directly opposite Busbys in Manningham Lane. 'Our Blushing Brides', starring Joan Crawford, was advertised for the following week, with Laurel and Hardy in a supporting film. Those were the days when a short film and the news were shown along with the 'big picture' - you certainly got your money's worth back then! Queues that formed outside the Theatre Royal began at the doors and snaked along the front of the building and down the hill. It showed its last film in 1974 - 'The Graduate,' starring Dustin Hoffman.

More Memories of BRADFORD II

The Hart & Clough story

It was 1885 when George Hart, who was a compositor with W N Sharpe Ltd, decided to leave his job and go into business on his own account. It was a key decision that was to prove a turning point in his life.

On 15th July 1885 he was offered the tenancy of Room 26 at 21 Swaine Street, Bradford at a rent of £17.00 a year, which was to be paid quarterly. Two double gas brackets and a gas meter were all the single room contained, but George Hart moved in and confidently set up his small printing business. Joseph Town & Sons paper manufacturers supplied George Hart with his initial stationery supplies, and the company, today known as Wiggins Teape Ltd, continues to supply Hart & Clough to this day.

Mr Hart's choice of premises was a shrewd one as Swaine Street was convenient for the Wool Exchange. From the early 1800s Bradford had been recognised as the centre of the worsted industry and the Wool Exchange, with its hundreds of subscribers, was one of the world's most important markets. With the wool merchants as its main clients, Mr Hart's printing business flourished and three years later he was ready to expand into an adjoining room. On March 15th 1888, for the additional rent of £8 a year - a mere three shillings a week - he took over Room 27 and the small cupboard it contained, though the few alterations that were needed to adapt the room to his purpose cost him an extra 15 shillings. In today's currency - though definitely not in value - 15 shillings is 75 pence.

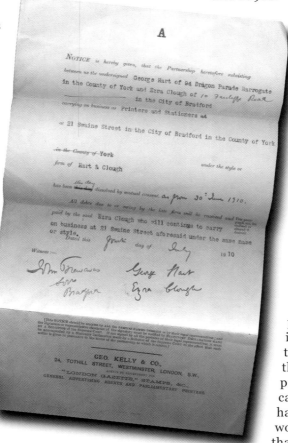

Top left: *Ezra Clough.*
Top right: *An early letterhead.*
Above centre: *The dissolution of the partnership between Ezra Clough and George Hart which allowed Ezra Clough to continue the business on his own.*

Back in 1888 it would have represented nearly five weeks' rent on the new room!

A few days later Mr Hart was joined in the business by Ezra Clough. Mr Clough knew the stationery business inside out, having been the manager of the Bradford stationery shop owned by J Y Knight & Co. The business became Hart & Clough, printers, in the mid 1890s.

Outside working hours Ezra Clough was developing a new hobby - photography. The camera had been invented a mere 70 or so years earlier by a French doctor, who in 1826 produced the world's first images from nature on pewter plates with a camera obscura and an eight-hour exposure. The new invention received the royal seal of approval when Queen Victoria posed for her first photograph in 1860. By the end of the century the techniques of photography had progressed in leaps and bounds from the camera obscura! In 1889 the Eastman Company produced the Kodak No 1 camera and roll film, giving hand-held snapshots to the world. It is hardly surprising that Ezra Clough became absorbed in his new hobby.

Fortunately for us he took his skills into the workplace, where in 1897 he proudly recorded images of the machine room and stockroom for

More Memories of **BRADFORD II**

posterity. A number of the fine photographs he took of the Hart & Clough premises in the late 1890s still survive, giving us a rare opportunity to slip back through time and view the old printing presses and equipment, the fixtures and fittings, and the stockroom neatly stacked from floor to ceiling with reams of paper, ledgers, notebooks, bottles of ink and a huge assortment of other stationery supplies. It is thanks to Ezra Clough's keen interest in photography that we have these fascinating images of how a small printing business operated in the late 19th century.

Above: *This picture was taken by Ezra Clough in 1897 showing a stockroom stacked from floor to ceiling with paper and card used in the printing and stationery business.*

More Memories of BRADFORD II

Ezra Clough became well known as an amateur photographer, and he eventually became President of the Bradford Photographic Society, a pioneer group of enthusiasts which had been founded in 1860. He was the first secretary of the Yorkshire Photographic Union - an association he helped to found in 1899 - and he held the post for an incredible 25 years. He would have been fascinated with Hart & Clough's camera, film-planning and platemaking departments that exist today! Coincidentally, Mr Percy Lund, who founded the well-known Bradford printers Lund Humphries Ltd, was the Yorkshire Photographic Union's first president. Lund Humphries was founded in the same year as Hart & Clough - 1885.

In August 1907 Ezra Clough's son, 16-year-old Frank Vincent, started work at Hart & Clough; the young man had no way of knowing, of course, that in joining the firm he had taken the first step towards establishing the business as the traditional family firm that it was eventually to become. Three years later George Hart retired, handing over the business to Ezra Clough.

Below: *Ezra Clough was an amateur photographer who took this photograph of the Machine Room in 1897.*

Young Vincent, meanwhile, was following in his father's footsteps and developing his own hobbies - though not photography. At the age of 18 he bought his own car and learned not only to drive it but to maintain it - a necessity in those early days of motoring when there were few cars about in Bradford, and fewer mechanics to mend them when they broke down. Building radio receivers was this young man's other passion. His aim was not to listen to popular music over the airwaves; radio programmes as we know them today were still in their infancy (the world's first radio programme of words and music had only been made four years earlier, in 1906, in the United States). It was in the Morse code messages from ships and from radio hams, the only transmissions at the time, that Vincent's interest lay. Morse code itself is now part of our past, as its use was discontinued in 1999.

As the First World War got into its stride, Hart & Clough acquired W H Butler, a Bradford bookbinding firm, re-launching it as Woods (Bradford) Ltd. The company was to become one of the most successful and prosperous trade binderies in West Yorkshire, and still continues so today.

Anxious to fight for his country, Vincent volunteered for military service and in 1916 was commis-

More Memories of BRADFORD II

sioned in the West Yorkshire Regiment. Before the war ended, however, he found himself back in Britain, seriously injured by shrapnel - and the piece that lodged in his knee was with him until his death. The incident could have been far worse, however; Vincent's silver cigarette case, which he carried in his breast pocket, stopped a piece of shrapnel that would otherwise have undoubtedly ended the young man's life prematurely. The cigarette case, complete with a large hole, is still treasured by his family, who value it as a rare piece of family history.

A key move was made in 1928, when Hart & Clough became an incorporated company, with Ezra and Vincent as directors. Ezra died six years later, just one year before his grandson Michael came into the company.

By the mid-1930s war once more loomed on the horizon. A need for more extensive premises was making itself felt, and the company moved to George Street. Some of the excellent work produced by Hart & Clough at the time has survived, notably a portfolio of elegant sample letterheads. Some of the designs are amazingly intricate, and the quality of the work demonstrates the skills of the designer and the printer.

When war was declared in 1939 Michael Clough was called up from the Territorial Army - and was closely followed by other members of staff who were within the age for military service. The older members were left to cope as best they could with a smaller workforce and a lack of skilled operatives, yet at the same time dealing with the need for increased production. The firm's van driver became one of those pressed into learning to operate a printing machine!

One of Hart & Clough's main clients during the war years was A V Roe, who built Lancaster bombers from their factory near Yeadon airport. When the war was

Above: *A sample of the company's colour printing expertise - a brochure produced for Listers of Manningham Mills, in 1964.*
Top: *The company's premises at George Street in the 1940s.*

More Memories of BRADFORD II

over they paid tribute to the work of Hart & Clough, recognising them as the printers who could always be depended on to deal with a rush job. 'Send it to Hart & Clough,' was the usual response to pressure of work - 'They'll get it through in time.' With the return of their staff from the services, Hart & Clough made a significant investment in new printing equipment, and also made another move into their present Summerville Road premises. The late 1940s and early 50s were a time of steady growth and a change of emphasis within the company from stationery production to brochures and publicity leaflets.

Those years brought significant changes in technology within the printing industry itself, and by 1952 Hart & Clough, determined to remain at the forefront, had installed its first lithographic offset press. It was to be the first of many.

Peter Clough, who is today's managing director, established the fourth generation of the family firm when he joined Hart & Clough in 1965 after graduating from the Printing College in Leeds. His first responsibility was to set up a camera and platemaking department. In 1969 the company's first Solna SRA2 litho machine was purchased, followed by another similar machine a couple of years later. The new investment in litho presses led eventually to an expansion in the camera, film-

Above: *An early 1980s exhibition where the company offered 'A complete service from design to delivery'.*

planning and platemaking departments.
New offices and a warehouse were added in 1980, the warehouse being built, owing to the soft nature of the land, on a 'raft' of steel reinforced concrete. Almost 2,000 square feet of floor space was needed for the building, and more than 150 tons of concrete and steel reinforcement were used.

At the same time other important renovations were made to the existing building in preparation for the installation of a four-colour Heidelberg GTO press. The new developments made it possible for the company to produce high quality colour printing at a very high speed.

The company made further advances in 1989, when they acquired The Amadeus Press, a specialist book and magazine printer based in Huddersfield. This proved to be a key move, establishing Hart & Clough as one of the leaders in short-run high quality book work. Today any print job can be taken on, from letterheads and business cards to packaging and full-colour books. In fact, the printing of this very book was undertaken by The Amadeus Press.

Computerisation was a necessary move within a company that was determined to keep abreast of modern technology and developments, and computers were brought into the everyday administration of Hart & Clough in the early 1980s. Some of the first software to be installed was an estimating programme developed and written by Michael Clough. In 1991 further developments were made with the introduction of the first computer-controlled four-colour press; a PC network was developed two years later for running the company's management information system (MIS). Richard Clough - the fifth generation of the family - joined the company after graduating from Manchester University Printing Course in 1993, making the completion of the computer network his responsibility. The introduction of an Apple Mac brought computerisation to yet another area of the factory, enabling designs and artwork for all items of printed matter to be created on screen. Well before the possibility of being overtaken by the 'Millennium bug', a completely new computer network and MIS system was installed in January 1999, ensuring a more streamlined processing of information within the company.

Over the years the company has established a solid philosophy of close involvement with clients while at the same time producing a first class job at a reasonable price - a tradition which will by the end of 1999 be enhanced by the acquisition of ISO 9002 accreditation.

The printing processes in general and Hart & Clough Ltd in particular have seen changes over the last 114 years that Ezra Clough could never have envisaged, when he gave his skills and his name to that small printing business so many years ago. The company's business philosophy of offering a high quality personal service, however, is one thing that has never changed - and it is Hart & Clough's aim to ensure that, as they move into the next millennium, that fundamental principle will remain the same.

Below: 2 + 4 colour Roland presses in operation at the Summerville Road premises in 1999.
Left: The Heidelberg 4-colour press installed in 1980.

More Memories of **BRADFORD II**

A sporting life

As we enter the new millennium it is pleasing to write that the outlook for the city's professional football and rugby clubs is particularly encouraging. This is in direct contrast with the experience of the last eighty years or so which was characterised more by a struggle for survival and ongoing financial difficulties. Sadly Bradford has lost one of its football clubs during this time (not to mention a popular stadium) and county cricket has also been lost to the city.

Nonetheless the photographs in this section testify to the fact that considerable progress has been made to ensure that Bradford will have sporting representatives of a status that is consistent with the size of the city. These images provide a sobering reminder of the struggles of Bradford's professional sports organisations and of the spectator facilities that existed (which appear relatively archaic to modern eyes). Despite the adversity and hardships there were many happy memories and moments of excitement.

Above: At the beginning of the 20th century Bradford was very much a rugby stronghold and the home to two founder members of what became the Rugby League. However the rivalry of Manningham and Bradford, based at Valley Parade and Park Avenue respectively, was unique in so far as they continued to be rivals in a different sport after their conversion to soccer. The Football League had been keen to establish soccer in the woollen district of the West Riding and this led to the formation of Bradford City AFC in 1903 and then Bradford AFC (often referred to as 'Park Avenue') in 1907. By the outbreak of war in 1914 both clubs were members of the first division and in 1911 City had achieved its greatest sporting achievement with the winning of the FA Cup. City's team photographed prior to the final in April, 1911 from left to right, rear: P.O'Rourke, Robinson, Campbell, Mellors, Taylor and Harper. Middle: Bond, Spiers, F.O'Rourke, Devine and Thompson. Front: Logan, Gildea and McDonald.

More Memories of BRADFORD II

Below: Bradford Northern RLFC, Bradford (Park Avenue) AFC and Bradford RFC (now merged with Bingley RUFC as Bradford & Bingley RFC) all share common genealogy that can be traced to the formation of Bradford RFC in 1863, one of the first rugby clubs in Yorkshire. This explains why each of the three clubs traditionally wore red, gold and black hooped shirts. The emergence of the Northern Rugby Union in 1895 had led to rival factions each supporting opposing rugby codes and establishing their own club structures. The subsequent formation of a football club at Park Avenue led to the formation of Bradford (Northern) in 1907 who adopted the Greenfield Stadium as its home (which was later used as a greyhound track). The club chose to add the suffix 'Northern' to its name to emphasise the fact that it was distinct from the football club of the same name and that an NRU side continued to play in the city. Bradford AFC subsequently referred to itself as Bradford (Park Avenue) to avoid any confusion with Bradford City. Featured left is the Bradford Northern side of 1924/25 at the Birch Lane ground where the club played between 1908 and 1934.

Bottom: The fortunes of both football clubs were subject to decline during the inter-war period with City and Park Avenue each losing their status as Division One sides. Bradford football derbies were contested in Division Two and Division Three (North) and football fans in the city looked on with envy as neighbouring Huddersfield Town enjoyed all the glory becoming the top side in the country. Bradford City and Bradford (PA) were each burdened with debt and in 1937 it was suggest that the clubs should merge and play at the new Odsal Stadium. However the supporters were anxious to preserve their separate identities and so a merger never took place. Bradford City had been relegated to the third division in 1937 and the club remained in the lower divisions for a further 48 years. In August 1938 a challenge match between the Bradford clubs was played at Valley Parade to mark the 50th anniversary of the Football League. The City team, from left to right: Smailes, Robertson, Comrie, Gore, McDermott, Moore, Murphy, Whittingham, Parker, Pallister and Goodyear.

More Memories of BRADFORD II

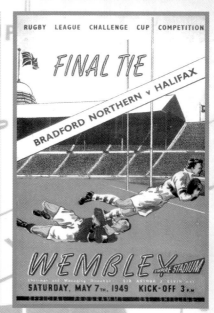

Above: The glory-era for Bradford Northern was undoubtedly the late forties when the club achieved a Wembley Treble with three successive appearances in the Challenge Cup Final in 1947, 1948 and 1949, winning the cup in 1947 and 1949. In 1948 the club finished as champions of the Yorkshire League and in 1952 as champions of the Northern League.

Above: The 1949 Cup winners are pictured from left to right: Tyler, Kitching, Foster, (Ernest) Ward, Traill, Batten, Whitcombe, Edwards, Greaves, Leake, Darlison, Davies and (Donald) Ward. Trevor Foster subsequently acted to safeguard the future of Bradford Northern in 1964 and indeed his name has been synonymous with the club for the last fifty years.

More Memories of BRADFORD II

Above: Odsal Stadium gained a place in the record books when an official crowd of 102,569 attended the Challenge Cup Final Replay in May, 1954. The potential for developing Odsal as the 'Wembley of the North' had been widely recognised and crowds of seventy thousand for big games were not uncommon. Ever since 1934, when the stadium had been created from the conversion of a municipal tip, various grandiose schemes had been discussed. Somewhat inevitably sufficient funds were not available to transform the bowl and to this day the potential of Odsal has never been realised. In addition to rugby Odsal was also home to speedway racing and the Australian promoter Johnny Hoskins was successful in attracting large crowds for the Saturday evening race nights. The Bradford track was regarded as one of the fastest in the country and Hoskins recruited some of the top riders. Dent Oliver, Oliver Hart and Joe Abbott were among the heroes of the Odsal team.

More Memories of BRADFORD II

Left: Odsal Stadium hosted soccer in the aftermath of the Bradford disaster but it was also the unlikely venue for a celebrity charity soccer match in March, 1960. The event was organised to raise funds for refugee relief and among the celebrities were Sean Connery and Tommy Steele.

Right: The immediate post-war history of City and Park Avenue was essentially a story of lower division football and recurring financial crises, reflecting in part the decline of the city's manufacturing base and general prosperity. Both clubs were desperately under-funded and enjoyed limited success. Nevertheless there were occasions of FA Cup glory such as the time when Bradford (PA), then a second division club, defeated the mighty Arsenal 1-0 at Highbury in January, 1948. Forty-eight thousand spectators witnessed Billy Elliott's goal but the Avenue team was then subject to a giant-killing when non-league Colchester beat Bradford in the next round. The following year eighty-three thousand people witnessed a 1-1 draw at Maine Road, Manchester as Bradford took on Manchester United. After another 1-1 draw however Avenue lost 0-5. The Bradford side that beat Arsenal became one of legend, from left to right standing: Henry, White, Hepworth, Farr, Farrell and Downie. Sitting: Smith, Ainsley, Greenwood, Elliott, Deplidge.

Bottom: Manager Peter Jackson led Bradford City to the fifth round of the FA Cup in the 1959/60 season. Having already defeated first division Everton the Bantams were drawn against champions-elect Burnley at Valley Parade. A capacity 26,227 crowd saw Robert Webb and Derek Stokes put City into a 2-0 lead with only 15 minutes remaining. Burnley pulled a goal back and then managed an equaliser in the final minute of injury time. City lost 0-5 in the replay at Turf Moor; the attendance for that game was 52,850 with a large contingent from Bradford and stories of traffic tailbacks as far as Shipley!

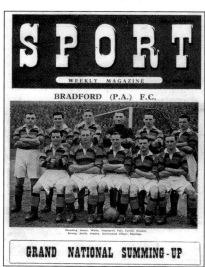

More Memories of BRADFORD II

Left: A comment on the state of Bradford football in the 1940's and 1950's is not complete without reference to the players sold by Park Avenue and City who subsequently achieved fame and fortune at the top of their profession elsewhere. These included the likes of former Paraders Sam Barkas at Manchester City, Joe Harvey at Newcastle (left) and Laurie Scott and George Swindin at Arsenal. Ex-Avenue men included Ron Greenwood at Brentford and Chelsea and Len Shackleton and Billy Elliott at Sunderland.

Centre left: The Valley Parade that existed in the 50s is unrecognisable from the stadium of today. Until the fire of 1985 Valley Parade remained essentially much the same as it had when it was redeveloped in 1908 upon City's promotion to Division One. The elegant Midland Road stand had been demolished in 1953 and for much of the next two decades the club operated with what was literally a three-sided ground. The fact that Valley Parade was built on a hillside had implications for building suitable foundations and finances dictated that the club was unable to redevelop the stadium. The Midland Road stand was not properly replaced until 1996 and in the meantime a series of small shelters were erected. The old Canal Road power station is visible in this photograph which features the game with Chesterfield in November, 1954.

Bottom: The Spion Kop and Main Stand are both full for the game with Mansfield in September, 1959. A dog appears to have entered the field of play to chase the ball!

More Memories of BRADFORD II

The general consensus among most Bradfordians was that Park Avenue was a better venue than Valley Parade and this was a debate which continued beyond the demolition of Park Avenue in 1980. There was little argument that the former enjoyed the better location and that the stadium at Park Avenue had better facilities. Especially after the demolition of the Midland Road stand in 1953 Valley Parade was a shabby ground. By contrast the Park Avenue complex had the Edwardian splendour of its cricket pavilion, the so-called Dolls House and the dual-sided grandstand that was shared by football and cricket spectators. The site of the old Horton Park railway station is evident at the bottom of this photograph which was taken in May, 1966. The station was closed in 1952 although the platforms had been kept intact for occasional football specials - of which there were few in the 60s! The line to City Road Goods Station can also be seen. Adjacent to the Park Avenue cricket ground is one of Bradford's first supermarkets operated by none other than WM Morrisons.

More Memories of BRADFORD II

Below: The Park Avenue cricket ground was regarded as one of the best playing surfaces in the country and it was always a popular venue for cricket lovers. Park Avenue was the home to Bradford Cricket Club, formed in 1836, and had played host to Yorkshire CCC fixtures since 1880. Brian Close (front centre) is pictured with the Yorkshire side at Park Avenue. In addition to being a fine cricketer Brian Close was also a good footballer and was on the books of Leeds and Arsenal before making his League debut with Bradford City in 1952; although he made only six appearances he nevertheless achieved a decent scoring rate with two goals!

Bottom: Bradford sport hit rock bottom during the sixties. City and Avenue both struggled at the bottom of Division Four and in fact it was only the fund-raising efforts of Bradford City supporters that prevented their club becoming extinct. Bradford Northern RLFC had similar financial problems and was obliged to resign from the Rugby League mid-way through the 1963/64 season although thankfully the club was reformed in time for the following season. Speedway at Odsal also closed down for a period. Meanwhile Bradford AFC set an unwanted record with only 15 wins out of 138 League games between 1967 and 1970. Many people traced the decline of the club to the sale of Kevin Hector to first division Derby County in September, 1966 although in reality the problems were much deeper rooted. Hector's strike partner at Park Avenue was Bobby Ham who was subsequently transferred across the city to Valley Parade and is remembered as one of the finest and most popular Bradford-born players. The Bradford (PA) team of 1967/68, from left to right rear: Hughes, Peel, Barnes, Hardie, Turner, I'Anson and Lightowler. Middle row: McBride, Burgin, Hibbit, Clancy and Ham. Front: Gould, Robinson and Lloyd.

More Memories of BRADFORD II

Top: The last League derby between Bradford City and Bradford (Park Avenue) was a goal-less draw at Park Avenue in January, 1969. Thus ended a long-standing rivalry that went back many generations. City were promoted at the end of that season to Division Three, the first time that the club had achieved promotion in forty years. By contrast, Bradford finished bottom of the League for the second season in succession and when the club repeated this feat again in 1970 there was little surprise that it failed to win re-election. Avenue continued in existence for another four seasons, vacating Park Avenue in 1973 and then sharing Valley Parade with City before succumbing to liquidation in May, 1974. Pictured in action during the derby at Park Avenue in September, 1967 is goalkeeper Pat Liney who had been transferred to Bradford City from Bradford earlier in the month.

Inset: Bradford's last League game at Park Avenue was against Scunthorpe United and appearing for the visitors that afternoon was Kevin Keegan, later to be transferred to Liverpool.

The result of the game was a resounding 0-5 defeat for the home side.

Above: In January, 1970 Valley Parade staged a third round FA Cup tie between Bradford City and Tottenham Hotspur. The game is remembered as one of the greatest Cup ties in Bradford with Bobby Ham and Bruce Stowell each scoring to secure a 2-2 draw but unfortunately City were crushed 0-5 in the replay at White Hart Lane.

More Memories of BRADFORD II

Below: Bradford AFC vacated Park Avenue is somewhat controversial circumstances and Avenue fans had strong feelings that Bradford Corporation did very little to assist the club. Park Avenue remained vacant and eventually became overgrown and heavily vandalised. At one stage in the mid seventies there was talk of rugby league being played at Park Avenue after more than sixty years. There were also proposals for the stadium to be used as a speedway venue although promoter Jim Streets was unable to convince local councillors of the benefits.

Bottom: The revival of Bradford Northern was marked in 1973 when the club reached Wembley for the final of the Challenge Cup. Featherstone, the favourites, won the game 33-14 despite a brave fightback by Northern. The 1972/73 squad, from left to right rear: Gallacher, Earl, Joyce, Long, Carlton, Fearnley, Small and Hogan. Middle: Jarvis, Redfearn, Stockwell, Cardiss, Tees (captain), Lamb, Pattinson, Watson and Brooke (coach). Front: Diabira, Blacker, Dunn, Treasure and Seabourne. Northern's achievement that year was in contrast to the poor showing of the city's football clubs with City languishing in the fourth division and Avenue in the Northern Premier League. How circumstances are now so very different compared to a quarter of a century ago!

More Memories of **BRADFORD II**

Bird's eye view

More Memories of BRADFORD II

Like arteries leading to the heart, this pattern of main roads - Manchester Road, Little Horton Lane and Morley Street - heads in towards Bradford city centre. The Odeon cinema - the Gaumont at the time of this photograph - stands in the lower left corner between New Victoria Street and Thornton Road. Readers who were in their teens in the 1950s will remember congregating with their mates in the Alassio Coffee Bar in New Victoria Street. The Alassio was the place to be seen if you were a 'cool cat' (and a good place to 'pull'!). Redevelopment was still in the future; the Photography Museum, the skating rink, the central library and the inner ring road were yet to be, and we still had the Princes Theatre, the Victoria Square roundabout, the Manchester Road Odeon and Chester Street bus station. The German Church (still with us) can be seen in Great Horton Road that rises towards the Bradford Institute of Technology, which in 1966 became the University of Bradford.

More Memories of BRADFORD II

Above: Is Shipley Station the only railway station in the country without a loo? Probably not, though it might seem so to those poor souls who have to wait for their train in acute discomfort! The modernisation of the old station, however, left Shipley with an otherwise fine facility. Shipley has gone through radical changes since this photograph was taken in the early 1950s. At the time, the 'new' Arndale building with its clock tower and downstairs market had not been built in Kirkgate, which runs horizontally across the centre of the photograph. A keen eye might pick out market stalls near the junction with Otley Road; Saltaire Road runs from the town centre towards the bottom right corner. Most of the area between Otley Road, Kirkgate and Manor Lane was swept away in the redevelopment scheme that gave Shipley a number of new flats, a pedestrianised shopping precinct and wide roads that keep the traffic flowing relatively smoothly.

Right: The most recognisable feature of this photograph is the Exchange Station with its twin arches, demolished in 1976. The road taking traffic across the railway lines nearest to the station is Bridge Street, and Croft Street, above it in the centre of the picture, is now a wide major thoroughfare linking Manchester Road with Leeds Road. Possessors of a keen eye will spot a number of archways behind the Victoria Hotel; these are all that remained of the cellars of the original Lancashire and Yorkshire Bonded Warehouse. Bradford Interchange today occupies this site.
Spot the Victoria Hotel and St George's Hall nearby, and the Telegraph & Argus building in its pre- glass extension days. The multi storey car park had been constructed in Hall Ings, though at the time this photograph was taken the Norfolk Gardens Hotel (now the Stakis) had yet to be built on the site that we see had already been cleared for it.

The Exchange Station, with its twin arches, was demolished in 1976

More Memories of **BRADFORD** *II*

More Memories of **BRADFORD** *II*

The Town Hall in the bottom right corner is the first (and to some perhaps the only!) recognisable feature of this eagle's-eye view of Bradford city centre. The photograph is undated, but as the Ritz Cinema still stands in Broadway it has to pre-date the cinema's closure in 1985. Market Street carries the eye forward from the Town Hall past the Wool Exchange directly to Forster Square Station, whose long buildings can be easily picked out at the top of the photograph. The view takes in most of Bradford's central shopping area, strangely flattening out the steep gradients of Ivegate, Queensgate and Darley Street. On the left readers will pick out the many-ridged roof of Kirkgate Market, where Bradfordians once spent many a happy shopping hour (remember those iron grilles set in the sloping floor that on cold days sent out a wonderful flow of warm air?). Those were the days.

More Memories of BRADFORD II

Above: Do you remember the old Rolarena? And the devastating fire that roared through the building in 1955? The fire, it is said, was so hot that tar melted on the roads, and the Fire Brigade could do little other than surround the largely wooden building with a curtain of cool spray. Traffic along Manningham Lane was, of course, brought to a complete standstill, bringing chaos and mayhem to the main Bradford-Keighley road. The Mecca dance hall eventually replaced the Rolarena, and those of us who were young during the 1960s remember many pleasant evenings spent waltzing, quickstepping - or downing a pint or two in the bar - at the Mecca. Dollars night club followed it, and today's youngsters dance to a different beat at The Maestro.

Valley Parade football stadium - a vastly different place in the 1950s - just edges into the left edge of the photograph; many changes have been made in recent years, and further new building is taking place there today. Valley Road Goods Yard lies to the left of Midland Road.

Right: Like Father Christmas in July, the new emerges conspicuously from the old, Wardley's angular boxes of Portland Stone sitting uncomfortably alongside Bradford's Victorian architecture. In the right corner of the photograph, work goes on apace in Hall Ings and Petergate on the building that was to house Tapp & Toothill stationery stores and Peter Lord's furniture shop. The domed roof of the Exchange Station just edges into the picture - its days were also numbered; built in 1880, the station was demolished in 1976. In nearby Broadway, C&A and the adjoining stores have been constructed, and cars are already filling up the rooftop car park. The Ritz Cinema - here the ABC - is still standing, as is the Swan Arcade, whose demolition in 1962-63 caused a public outcry. Even the voices of the celebrated J B Priestley and David Hockney, however, could not save it from what Priestley labelled 'Council vandalism'.

Today, Bradford Council is building up a good record in conservation, and the Paper Hall, the Wool Exchange and Little Germany are examples of what can be done to preserve the heritage we still possess.

More Memories of BRADFORD II

More Memories of **BRADFORD II**

Above: How many readers would know without being told that this countryside stadium set in the middle of green fields is Odsal Stadium in its earlier years? A far cry from today, when Rooley Avenue is often choked with traffic trying to reach the motorway, and many of these open fields are residential areas - not to mention the Richard Dunn Sports Centre!
Work began on building Odsal stadium during the 1930s. The new stadium had enormous potential as a crowd puller, and during the 1950s ambitious plans were devised that would give the ground an eventual capacity of 92,000, providing for extension to 100,000 if necessary. Some memorable games have been played over the years at Odsal, but on the 5th May 1954 that extra capacity was needed. Were you at the unforgettable Rugby League Cup Final replay between Halifax and Warrington? That match drew mega crowds of 102,569 - the official world record crowd, though it was suggested that the unofficial number could have been far higher, possibly even reaching a massive 150,000. The thrill of speed also drew fans in their thousands to Odsal to watch speedway, rooting for Eddie Rigg, Arthur Wright, Arthur Forrest and Max Grosskreutz, the Australian rider whose inspiration motivated his team to masterly performances. Perhaps you and your friends were among the crowd, sitting in the front rows? The view down there was brilliant - but the cinders that spat viciously from the bike wheels were no joke!

Right: Five Lane Ends (near the top edge of the photograph) should, as all locals know, be Six Lane Ends. Names, however, have a tendency to stick, and the old name was kept on even after Swain House Road added another junction to the busy roundabout when Swain House estate was built. Since the years between the two world wars, the building of new homes has been a priority in the Wrose area, and this 1953 photograph shows that new houses are still going up in the Low Ash and Thornacre Road areas to the left of Wrose Road, which meanders towards Idle through the centre of this bird's eye view. Readers might be able to pick out in the distance the line of Kings Road, opened by the Prince of Wales back in the 1930s before he became Edward VIII. Tucked out of sight among the trees in the right foreground are the Wrose Bull pub - remembered by a former resident as a 'cosy' establishment - and the Roman Catholic church, demolished only recently in 1998.

More Memories of **BRADFORD II**

More Memories of BRADFORD II

Main Street bisects this splendid view of Bingley, with the River Aire to the right and the Leeds and Liverpool Canal and the railway line to the left. The road itself has changed little - apart from in the volume of traffic using it, of course. The Aire Valley Trunk Road has been planned on paper for many years, and in readiness for the project the canal was some time ago moved towards the left (westward). Will it ever be built? we wonder. Other changes have been made since this photograph was taken. Land near Myrtle Park was cleared for the Bingley Building Society and for the nearby shopping precinct. Traffic lights were installed where the road forks, and a new fire station was built near the parish church; those who do not know Treacle Cock Alley alongside the graveyard should explore it just for the experience! Full of character, the old alleyway goes under the railway - once lit by a single gas lamp - through the allotments and up to Three-Rise Locks.

More Memories of **BRADFORD II**

Down at the shops

'Attention! Busbys Sale!!' screams the poster on the wall, and scurrying shoppers hurry to the store by car, bus, tram and on foot in search of a bargain. The building on the far right of the photograph is the Girls Grammar School, which was acquired by Busbys in the late 1940s; they then extended the store to Hallfield Road. They also opened the nearby Fountain Hall, which proved to be a popular venue for wedding receptions, balls, meetings and functions. After working as a team with his sons for around 40 years, Ernest Busby died in 1957.

Trams were seen around the city as early as 1882, when a horse-drawn tram service operated along this section of road between Rawson Square and Lister Park. Electric trams were introduced in 1898. Lovers of trivia will enjoy learning that between 1917-18 three rifles, two gas ovens and a dog were among the three thousand-plus items left behind on trams in the city. Umbrellas, yes. But gas ovens? Imagine the scene. Irate wife: 'So where's my new gas oven?' Careless husband: 'Oh dear, I left it on the tram....' We are left wondering how he got it on the tram in the first place....

More Memories of BRADFORD II

Above: The curve of the tramlines follows Cheapside past the station and into Forster Square in this mid-1920s scene of the city centre. There are more pedestrians around than cars, though a number of delivery wagons, both motorised and horse-drawn, are making their way - it would appear rather haphazardly - around the square. The single motor cycle and sidecar bring back memories; when did you last see one of these? A traffic policeman, distinguished by his white gloves, keeps them all in order, though the people happily milling around in the roadway would have been more difficult to control!
The Midland Hotel to the left of the photograph still plays an active part in Bradford life, but the buildings on the right, part of a triangular block, were demolished. It is interesting to note that at the time the well known Bradford jewellers Fattorini's had premises here at the end of Kirkgate, and that they were 'makers to the Admiralty', supplying nautical instruments. The company was founded by John Enrico Fattorini in Manchester Road in 1912; the enterprising businessman also offered goods by mail order. After joining forces with Sydney Owthwaite, the successful venture went on to become the Bradford mail order giant, Grattan.

Right: Busby's clock tells us that it is twenty to ten, and Manningham Lane bustles with morning shoppers and traffic. Most of the shoppers, of course, are patronising Busbys, a favourite store with all 'old' Bradfordians. How we enjoyed browsing among its fashions and menswear, watches and jewellery, cosmetics and accessories! Bradford has had a Busbys store since 1908, when after serving a strictly-regimented apprenticeship with Matthew Rose, a linen draper in Middlesex, Ernest William Busby opened his first shop in Kirkgate. Rose had labelled Ernest Busby 'the best apprentice he'd ever had', and when Busby opened his first shop that expertise showed.
The shop never failed to show a profit, and in 1930 Busby moved out to the Manningham Lane premises, where he opened new departments including the famous restaurant. Nine years later, his staff numbered an incredible 800. From the department store's early days there had been friendly links between Busbys and Debenhams, and in 1953 the two firms merged voluntarily. By 1961 the store was serving 80,000 customers a week, and that same year it underwent an entire refit. As we know, Debenham's was doomed; fire raged through the building in 1979, and the store disappeared from the Bradford map.

More Memories of BRADFORD II

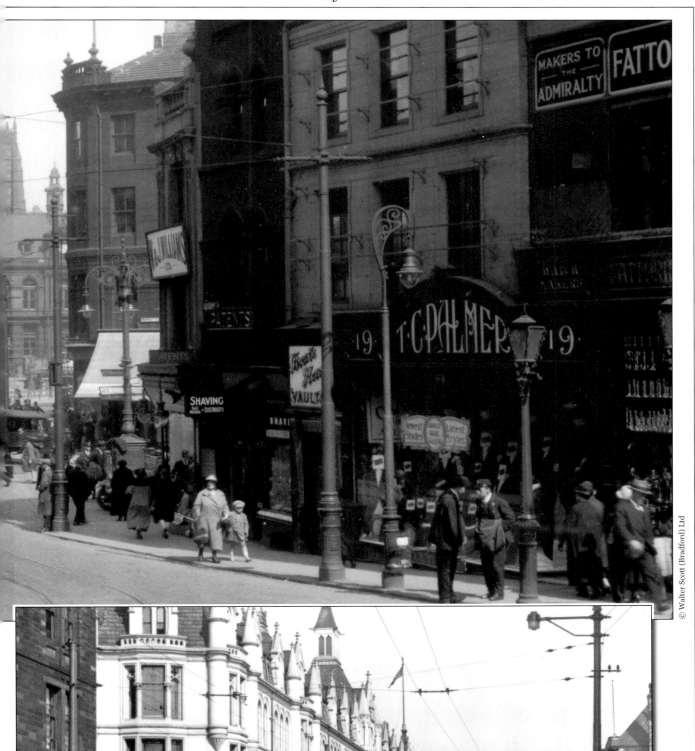

More Memories of BRADFORD II

A busy day in Manningham Lane, which even in the mid 1930s carried a large amount of heavy traffic. A lorry piled insecurely with bales of wool (can we detect a slight list to port?) heads away from Bradford on the main Keighley road, while a long line of cars travels towards the town centre. This same spot is unrecognisable today; growing traffic levels call for new roads, and Drewton Street and Hamm Strasse (still known to many as 'that there new road') now meet at this point.

The Regent Cinema, better known to most Bradfordians as the Essoldo (the name changed in 1950) was only one of a number of cinemas in the town centre; more than one reader will perhaps remember holding hands with their first boy or girl friend on the back row of the Essoldo. Sadly, this rather ornate building disappeared along with the Theatre Royal on the other side of the road, and Busbys, for many years one of Bradford's favourite department stores.

© Walter Scott (Bradford) Ltd

More Memories of **BRADFORD II**

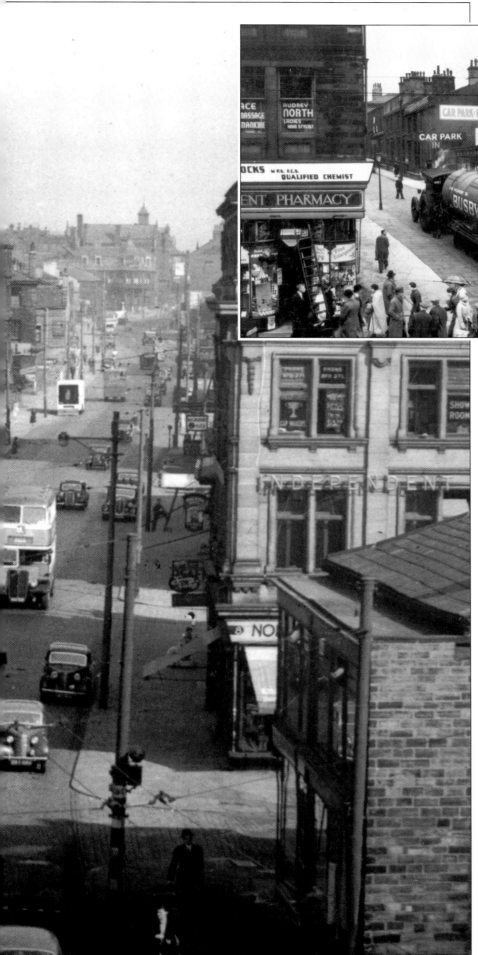

Above: Drawn by steam traction engine, the first of two enormous new boilers destined for installation in Busbys' basement arrives at the store. The second boiler was delivered the following day, ensuring that a constant supply of power for the central heating system and laundry could be generated on the premises. This photograph will remind older Bradfordians that Busbys not only had car parking facilities at the rear of the building, but they also sold petrol.
Busbys moved to Manningham Lane in 1930 when their premises in Kirkgate became too small for the rapidly growing company. The department store dominated the city end of Manningham Lane for many years, and our readers will remember with affection Busbys 'four soldier' logo. To the company's founder Ernest Busby the four marching soldiers were a symbol of unity, progress, uprightness and forward movement. The store offered customers an enormous range of goods and services, including at one time a modern furnished bungalow that displayed their large range of furniture and equipment in an appropriate setting.

More Memories of BRADFORD II

Bottom: We have no date for this photograph, but we can make a guess that it was some time in the 1950s. The family walking along Tyrrel Street are nicely reflected in the glass of Burtons window, reminding us that the famous menswear shop was once situated here. The shop on the opposite corner of Aldermanbury we believe to have been a greengrocers for many years; was this the business, we wonder, referred to by the sign above the doorway that proudly informs us, 'Established 1855'? A web of trolley bus wires leads along Tyrrel Street, and an informative sign across the road tells us helpfully that the Number 47 trolley to Little Horton passes St Luke's Hospital. Motor buses bound for Canterbury Avenue used the same stop. In spite of the bus stops, parking seems to have been allowed just here. Is that an old Ford Popular on the right? More than one reader will remember its frustrating vacuum windscreen wipers that stopped when you put your foot down and flogged away like mad when you took your foot off the accelerator!

Right: This interesting view along Market Street gives us an unfamiliar clear view of the hillside that rises to Wapping and Bolton Road. What would we see if we stood on the same spot today? We would of course be standing in Centenary Square, laid down in 1997 to commemorate the signing of the Royal Charter by Queen Victoria in July 1897 that created the City of Bradford. The buildings on the right of the photograph were later demolished; interestingly the antique shop on the corner appears to have been named 'Ann Teeke'!

Readers will perhaps remember the Clock mounted on the building that gave us 'Guinness Time'. The British public have believed that Guinness was good for them since the drink was first advertised in 1929. Many clever slogans have been produced over the years: 'Tall, Dark and Have Some', 'Seven Million Every Day and Still Going Down' and notably 'I've Never Tried it Because I Don't Like it'. And remember 'Guinness is Good for you - Just think what Toucan do'?

The huge Singer advertisement with its hand-operated sewing machine mounted on the opposite corner was just as familiar to Bradfordians for many years.

More Memories of **BRADFORD II**

This 1940s photograph captures shoppers entering and leaving the ever-popular Kirkgate Market Hall, whose floor actually sloped to follow the contour of the hill it was built on. Older Bradfordians might remember Hilda Lincoln's flower stall, its containers of daffodils and tulips (or roses and chrysanthemums, according to the time of year) - the first cheerful sight that greeted the eye as you entered the door at the top of the steps from Kirkgate. You could buy virtually anything from the market hall: handbags, shopping bags and purses, dolls, skipping ropes and mouth organs, hats, dresses, aprons and jewellery, books old and new - and a couple of shillings would buy you the sheet music of the latest popular song.

You could sit on tall stools and enjoy a dish of ice cream, a fruit-flavoured milk shake, or a cup of coffee on a cold day. And if you felt like eating something more substantial you could order mouth-watering pork pies and mushy peas at an establishment known to our grandparents as 'Pie Tom's'.

Bradford has had its markets ever since the 11th Century. Have any of them been as well loved and missed as Kirkgate Market, we wonder?

The floor of the Kirkgate Market actually sloped to follow the contour of the hill it was built on

More Memories of BRADFORD II

Doesn't it seem strange to see traffic in what is now a pedestrian precinct? They say that we don't value a thing until we lose it, and maybe that's true of Darley Street. How many of these busy passers-by lifted their eyes above shop window level to admire the Kirkgate building's Victorian elegance? Modern concrete has today replaced the old building, but nevertheless the view is still recognisable. Kirkgate Market's side entrance is half way up the street on the left. Darley Street has always been one of Bradford's most important shopping streets, with a wide range of shops and facilities. At the time the city was graced by Woolworth's, up the hill on the right, which disappeared from the city a number of years ago. Situated next door below Marks and Spencer, the much-loved Woolies was replaced by fashion shops. Younger readers might be surprised to read that Bradford's Central Library was in Darley Street, on the left near the top of the hill.

More Memories of BRADFORD II

More Memories of BRADFORD *II*

More Memories of BRADFORD II

Left: Rawson Market had an atmosphere of its very own, didn't it? The subtle scents of oranges and apples competing with the sharper odours of onions and leeks.... You could buy more than fruit and vegetables there, however: cheese, flowers, meat and game, while fish had an entire market (with its own unsubtle odours!) all to itself.

Bradford got off lightly during the war, but Rawson Market was one of the few casualties of Nazi bombs. The western end of the market hall was completely destroyed during a lengthy air raid on the night of 31st August 1940. Thirty-two stalls inside the market, plus seven street-facing shops, were completely gutted. The Fish Market in James Street came to the rescue and found places for the displaced fruit stalls. The market was not rebuilt for many years after the war owing to lack of funds, and it was 1958 before the first phase of the work was completed. Phases two and three followed in 1959.

Below: Road works have been part and parcel of Bradford life since tarmac was invented, though perhaps these workmen would today have been wearing hard hats. In the 1950s road works were the only real changes Bradford had seen, and our impressive Victorian buildings were still intact. Even wartime air raids had left most of the town centre untouched - a situation that was about to be 'remedied' by Stanley Wardley, who was appointed as the city's engineer and surveyor in 1946. The Kirkgate Market building, stately and elegant even with its covering of soot, was just one of our beautiful Victorian buildings that fell victim to Wardley's clean sweep of the late 1960s and 70s. The carved stone from the market entrance was removed to lie in ignominy in Lister Park. Darley Street was (and still is) Bradford's main shopping street, and Alexandre 'Executive Tailoring' was a familiar sight on this corner, with Kinos furriers occupying the adjacent property. Fur was still very much a fashion statement in the 1950s before the tide of public opinion turned against the wearing of genuine fur.

More Memories of BRADFORD II

Above: This particular lamp standard surrounded by four bollards had shed light on the junction of Market Street, Kirkgate and Cheapside for many decades, though this 1960s photograph shows that the ornate top with its four arc lamps of earlier years has been replaced by two modern lights. This triangular block of buildings on the corner of Kirkgate was later demolished. Kerbside parking is in practice here - not a yellow line in sight! It is interesting to note the police officer on point duty; there was a time when every major junction in every major town had its traffic 'bobby'. A sharp eye might spot a second officer further up Kirkgate in his black and white zebra-striped box. The boxes made the police officers highly visible and gave them the elevation and air of authority they needed. One by one they disappeared, leaving us with a trail of traffic lights at every major road junction - including this one. Efficient the computerised lights may be, but somehow they lack the personal touch of the good old traffic bobby.

Above right: What a marvellous display of mouthwatering goodies! It was 1951, and Bradford Markets were 700 years old - an event that deserved the very best in celebrations.
This confectioner in Kirkgate Market had really gone to town on his superb display, grouping his sweets and chocolates, Mars, Nestle's, Wilkinsons, Cadburys and all the rest, into a real work of art

beneath portraits of Kings Henry III and George VI and the Bradford coat of arms. What a pity we can't read the confectioner's name, which has sadly been forgotten. Perhaps some reader will remind us!
King Henry III, looking very majestic in his crown and robes, had back in 1251 granted to Edmund de Lacy 'and his heirs for ever' a Charter for markets to be held in Bradford. Kirkgate, opened in 1878, was the latest in a long line of markets, and the architects Lockwood and Mawson combined the best of Europe's elegant buildings into its design. The year 1951 saw a double celebration, as the Festival of Britain that commemorated the Great Exhibition of 1851 was in full swing across the country at the time.

Right: Steadily falling rain emphasises the desolation of another group of fine buildings awaiting the bulldozer, and Timms & Dyason's window, with its lovely pane of curved glass, stands empty and abandoned on the corner of Bridge Street. A tell-tale notice beneath the pillars stresses the reason: 'Expiration of lease'. Nearby in Market Street are other vacated shops and businesses that needed to find alternative premises; these include the Silver Grill, Davies & Balmforth, and a branch of Brown Muff. They have all had their closing down sales and departed, and the empty buildings stand ready for demolition. Work has already started on the building beyond Barclays Bank; interestingly, the bank was the only building in the block to survive. Barclays relinquished this building in recent years, and it is now The Old Bank pub, where the clink of glasses and the buzz of conversation is more likely to be heard than the quiet rustle of banknotes being counted.

Most of us hated to see so many of our old buildings go. In 50 years or so, will a future generation of Bradfordians campaign against the demolition of *their* heritage - the Arndale Centre, perhaps, or C&A?

Below: The changing face of Bradford: here, the much-loved Swan Arcade has been reduced to ground level, and future years would see Stead & Simpson shoe shop occupying this particular corner site. On the opposite side of Broadway, the construction of new buildings is in progress, and this scaffolded building would eventually become Burger King. The Ritz Cinema is just off-picture to the right, but would itself soon fall prey to the hungry bulldozer. The redevelopment that wiped out huge areas of the city centre brought advantages in the form of large stores such as C&A, which has over the years established itself in people's affections. Next door is W H Smith, with British Home Stores on the corner. Boots the Chemists' premises extended through from Charles Street into Broadway. Mothercare moved into the building when Boots relocated, though eventually Mothercare cut down the size of their store, leaving the Charles Street part to be taken over by other traders.

More Memories of BRADFORD II

Bradfordians who are into alternative medicine will remember and still miss Mitchells Chemists in Darley Street. Alongside their provision of conventional medication, Mitchells also dispensed homeopathic remedies to those who prefer to treat their ailments without the use of drugs. The Electricity showrooms and service centre eventually moved from these adjoining premises, though the move took them only a few yards. Their large showroom occupied a place on the opposite side of Darley Street for a number of years. Many of the businesses at the top end of Darley Street have today given way to charity shops, with at least four in this particular stretch of roadway. Though despised by some, charity shops are a treasure trove for bargain hunters and a lifeline for the city's unemployed.

Motor buses were an unfamiliar sight in Darley Street, as this was not part of a regular bus route. This one is out of service, however, and is bound for an unknown destination. The two-tone Triumph Herald on the right will be of interest to motoring enthusiasts; note its distinctive rectangular spotlamps that were characteristic of the mid-1960s - a fact that helps us to date this photograph. Traffic here is now one-way - in the other direction.

> *Alongside more conventional medicines, Mitchells dispensed homeopathic remedies*

More Memories of **BRADFORD II**

Above: Before self-service shopping began to catch on the corner shop was a part of everyone's life, and 'running errands' provided pocket money for many a child of the 1940s and 50s. John Hirst's shop on the corner of North Street and Fountain Street in Low Moor was only one of several sweet shops, grocers and greengrocers in the close-knit community. First and foremost, Hirst's was a sweets and tobacco shop, but you could buy much more than that there. Packets of firelighters and bundles of firewood bound with wire, cans of food, biscuits displayed in wonderful old tins with glass tops, shoe laces, buttons and thread, and even hair nets! A lending library was added to the shop's attractions in the mid 1950s, the old books regularly changed for different ones by Foyles, who ran the library service. Behind a curtained-off area lay John Hirst's other service to the community - his small printing press on which he turned out beautifully-presented letter-heads and business cards. The letter 'H' had a special use; readers who were children during the 1950s might remember that if they bought a penny ice lolly that turned out to have the letter 'H' embossed on the stick, they could claim another one free of charge!

Top: Instantly recognisable to those who use the main Keighley Road regularly is Avondale Buildings. The date given for this photograph is 1929, and amazingly at least two of the businesses have the same use today. Jowetts grocer's shop on the corner is now a mini market and off-licence, and though the titles sold might have changed, the newsagent further along the row still dispenses news to the local residents. Enormous changes, however, came to the rest of these little shops. The electrical dealer Peter Dyer has occupied a number of these properties for many years - though the firm is set to move premises in 1999. Avondale Motors has the shop at the far corner, with Kutts barber's shop and a large pizza takeaway in between.

At one time every small community had its own small shops, with greengrocers, butchers, bakers and grocers giving friendly and personal service to local people. In those early days goods such as biscuits, sugar and dried fruit were all weighed out for the individual customer. People might have had to wait a while longer to be served, but at least they had the benefit of one-to-one attention from the staff.

More Memories of **BRADFORD II**

Fares, please!

More mature readers will remember the days when tramlines were still in place on many of our main roads. Their days were numbered, however, and it was a foregone conclusion that despite the occasional alarming newspaper headline ('Motorbus thrill - fire under driver's seat'), motor buses would eventually replace them.

The year 1958 saw the Transport Department's Diamond Jubilee, and to mark the occasion the public were offered a taste of nostalgia; sixpence would buy you a blue ticket for a tram ride that ran the length of the yard at Thornbury Works, sadly the only place where tram lines remained. This became an occasional though regular service that usually operated on the anniversary of the demise of tram services, and as can be seen from the photograph the event was very popular with visitors. Unfortunately the novelty tram track in Thornbury yard was poorly maintained; one day there was a big bang and a blue flash - then nothing. The earth return had corroded, bringing an end to the nostalgic route.

More Memories of BRADFORD II

Above: The Number 29 was a cross-city service that linked Bradford Moor to Heaton via the city centre; this Number 29 tram was snapped in Wilmer Road, Heaton. The first electric tramcar ran in the city as long ago as 1892, when an experimental track was laid from Forster Square up Cheapside to Manningham Lane. They found, however, that the trams did not have enough power to pull up the hill when loaded. Bradford power station could only produce 300v, while to operate efficiently the trams needed 500v. (Wouldn't you think they would have found this out first of all?) Back to the drawing board.... Bradford had its trams until 1950. The last route to go was Odsal and Horsfall Playing Fields. The redundant trams suffered various fates. Many sadly went to the breaker's yard, but the top decks of Numbers 89 and 223 became greenhouses in Great Horton allotments; 127 became a bungalow on Baildon Moor, 31 was turned into a tool shed while 104 became a scoreboard at Odsal Stadium and was later preserved.

Top: Rush hour traffic in the 1930s was not quite what it is today, though two police officers are on point duty in Forster Square. A Number 26 tram heads out towards Baildon Bridge, and more trams are expected judging by the length of queues under the shelters in the background. Though there were a large number of private cars about at the time, the vast majority of people travelled by public transport. For most families, owning a car was just a pipe dream that rarely became a reality until the 1950s post-war prosperity. The main Post Office, with the Cathedral behind it, forms a soot-grimed backdrop to the photograph, while to the left is Forster Square LMS Station and further along, the premises of the YMCA, which was demolished some 30 years later along with the adjoining warehouse. Note the huge expanse of cobbled roadway and imagine the manpower needed to lay these granite setts!

Right: This interesting picture raises more questions than it answers! We have to wonder first of all what a Number 29 Chelmsford Road trolley bus is doing in Thornton Road, well away from its route and a number of miles away from its eventual destination in Bradford Moor. Secondly we would want to know why it is parked on this corner at an angle that would present at least a partial obstruction to oncoming traffic. A group of three men, one of whom appears to be the bus conductor, are just rounding the corner of a building advertising tyres; this building no longer exists, though you can still purchase a set of new tyres near this same spot at ATS. The triangular block of buildings behind the bus is still there and still provides motorists driving from Grattan Road into Listerhills Road with a 'rat run' that avoids the traffic lights at the Thornton Road junction. This little newsagents and cafe at one time offered a valuable service to the many firms in this largely industrial area, though the cafe's rather desolate air might indicate that the photograph was taken after it had closed down. A little cafe still operates further along the block.

Below: The Town Hall clock informs us that it is ten past five, and at the end of this working day a longish queue of office and shop workers waits for the number 37 Clayton trolley bus behind the New Inn in Thornton Road. A fascinating scale of fares at the terminus indicates that fares were affordable, even for the times; the three-mile ride to Clayton cost only twopence-halfpenny, and children could ride for three-halfpence. In those days, however, children were expected to stand and give up their seats to adults; you don't often see that nowadays!

A belisha beacon on the left indicates that a pedestrian crossing exists at this point, though zebra stripes have not yet been introduced. With the exception of one woman, however, most people seem to be ignoring it. Halford's cycle shop occupied this position on the corner of Thornton Road for many years.

More Memories of **BRADFORD II**

Above: Passers-by glancing casually at this scene would assume, naturally enough, that this trolley bus is going to Buttershaw, which is the destination on the blind. But hang on a minute - the route number alongside the destination is 45, which anyone who regularly travelled this way could have told you was Wibsey. The bus driver, however, knew where he was going, and in the end that is all that really mattered. We have no doubt that this young lady waiting at the bus stop eventually arrived safely at her destination. In the background readers will recognise the Unitarian church which had Channing Hall alongside; they may even remember attending concerts in the Hall, or perhaps even playing in one. Channing Hall was the kind of venue much beloved by music teachers for the occasional concert held to display their pupils' skills on the piano (and maybe bring in an extra bob or two!). Both the church and the hall had to go in the name of progress, and the Princes Way development today occupies the site where worshippers once gathered week by week and youthful pianists picked their way determinedly through 'Fur Elise'.

Top: In the mid 1960s pedestrian precincts were undreamed of at this spot where Tyrrel Street meets Sunbridge Road, the turning place for Duckworth Lane and Allerton trolley buses. The Duckworth Lane service was unbelievably efficient; at peak periods a Number 8 trolley left every two-and-a-half minutes! Traffic lights were in operation at the junction, though a number of intrepid souls obviously didn't care whether the lights were green or red as long as they got home in time for tea.... The feet of shoppers and, of course, the city's pigeons, now rule this area. If we were allowed a glimpse to the right and left we could look up Sunbridge Road towards Sunwin House on the left, while to the right we would see the well-known optician Butterfields, and Stead & Simpson's three-floor shoe shop. Gents' footwear were on the ground floor, ladies' on the first and children's on the third. Further along Tyrrel Street is the well-loved Brown Muff store which eventually became Rackhams. A 1965 Ford Anglia (well remembered for its distinctive rear window) is about to turn into Sunbridge Road, and readers will recognise as a Triumph Herald the vehicle travelling towards us along Tyrrel Street.

More Memories of BRADFORD II

Bottom: Trolley bus Number 844 is in trouble, and fortunately for the driver and the repair crew the roads are very quiet. Stranded at the Toller Lane and Duckworth Lane junction, the driver on the Number 8 Duckworth Lane route had to call for help in the form of the tower wagon. Overhead workers are beavering away at bus top level, and the trolley booms above them look quite forlorn, splayed at an awkward angle. It would not be long, however, before the bus was back on the road and ready to pick passengers up again. The tower wagon would perhaps not have had too far to come to this particular job, as the Duckworth Lane bus depot is not too far away.

Glory came to this very bus on Sunday 26th March 1972 when 844 was chosen to become Bradford's - and Britain's - very last trolley bus. On the Big Day crowds were gathering outside Duckworth Lane depot as early as four o'clock in the morning, saddened to see the old trolleys go but determined to be there at the end. Trolleys were filled all day, and many enthusiasts were stranded in Bradford when the final trolley left for Thornton at 10.57pm with 76 passengers - the maximum load.

Right: Public transport is almost the only traffic moving along Thornton Road as two Number 7 trolley buses pass each other on their cross-city journey between Thornton and Thornbury. Buses have long acted as very effective mobile advertising hoardings, and the trolley heading out towards Thornton is advertising Bradford's main Austin dealers, the Central Garage in Town Hall Square. On the right of this photograph advertisements for Laveracks DIY in Manchester Road (remember their special storm proof thresholds?), and for the Daily Mail's women's magazine 'Femail', are mounted on the boundary fence that separated passers-by from the nearby construction site. The open space in the background is the Sunwin House car park, which still survives.

Today at this spot traffic lights control the wide roadways of Thornton Road, Godwin Street and Princes Way, which carry an increasingly heavy load of traffic around the periphery of the city. A combination of new roads and pedestrianised areas has done much to open up the city centre to the shopping public, who no longer have to take their lives in their hands to cross Darley Street.

More Memories of **BRADFORD II**

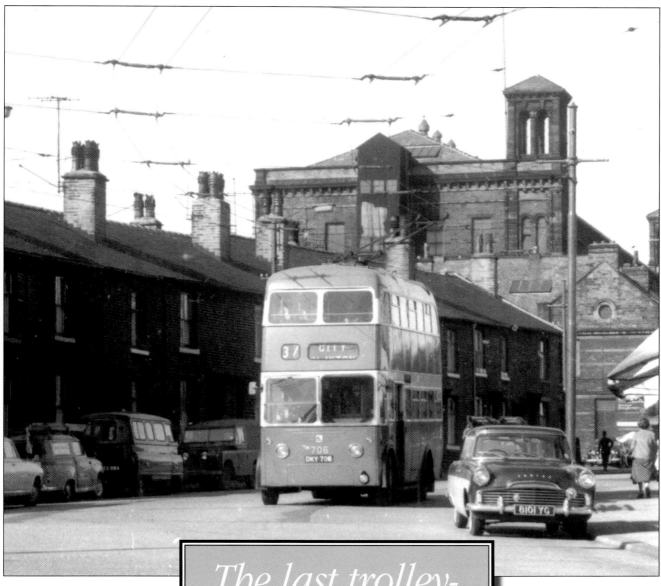

The last trolley-bus ran in Bradford on Sunday 26th March 1972

Motorists among our readers will remember shopping for spares and accessories at Merricks Stores on the right of Listerhills Lane; perhaps the driver of this Ford Zodiac has popped in for a new set of spark plugs! A number of interesting old vehicles are parked on the left: a Vauxhall estate car, an Austin A35 van, the larger Morris J4 van and an old-style Land Rover. The building with the small towers in the background is Ickringill's Mill, which today is shared by a number of firms.

A Number 37 trolley heads towards the city from Clayton; the Number 36 also went to Clayton, though by a slightly different route; a mile or so outside the village the Number 37 took the left branch up Pasture Lane while the Number 36 followed Bradford Road and The Avenue. Clayton roundabout is traditionally the site of the old 'wells' horse-troughs, an important landmark to Claytonians. After being at one time removed they were later replaced by popular demand - though the wrong way round. The roar of the diesel bus eventually replaced the quiet purr of the smooth-running trolley, on this as on all Bradford routes. On Sunday 26th March 1972 the last trolley bus ran in Bradford.

More Memories of **BRADFORD II**

Outskirts

The seat on The Green in Idle; a great place to sit and have a natter with an old friend - or just to sit and watch the world go by. Some things in life change very little, The Green being one of them, and the seat on The Green is still giving today's residents the same pleasure as it gave those of 60 years or so ago. Always a close community, the village has long offered its residents a good selection of local shops and services. The biggest changes in Idle, of course, began with the closing of the railway line, and the bridge at the bottom of High Street disappeared from the landscape long ago. The line ran from Bradford Exchange through Fagley and Eccleshill to Idle, then with a sweep to the left, travelled on to Shipley and Windhill. The railway line, as we know, was put to good use, giving the village the new road it badly needed. The old station was eventually demolished, making way for Dunns - a store that was to attract shoppers into Idle from all around the city.

More Memories of BRADFORD II

Below: We could easily use this unfamiliar view to play the game 'Where is it?'; how many readers have recognised this scene as Apperley Bridge? The A658, Harrogate Road, stretches away in front of us towards the open countryside, an area of fields, woods and empty hillsides. Many of the fields and trees are still there of course, but the long hillside before us is now lined with houses on the left and business premises on the right. At the bottom of the hill near the junction with Apperley Road a filling station and a pleasant pub cater for the needs of both the motorist and his (or her) car. Highways of a different kind pass beneath the road; in the valley Harrogate Road crosses both the River Aire and the Leeds and Liverpool Canal.

This pleasant area on the slopes of the hill below Rawdon boasts the prestigious Woodhouse Grove school and its prep department, Bronte House. The neighbouring sewage works is tucked well out of sight, preserving the beauty of the countryside. The works themselves, however, are proving to be of real interest, and hundreds of Bradfordians descend on the facility on their all too rare open days.

Bottom: The Fleece pub in Main Street was quenching the thirst of local Bingley residents back in 1928, though the attraction of satellite television was a delight that then lay many years in the future! This section of roadway has, apart from the addition of traffic lights at the junction, seen few changes in living memory; some readers will even remember the days when trams ran to Bingley and Cottingley.

Many years ago, however, this road was very different. The main road, very narrow at the time, once went off to the left and wound around these cottages, leaving the parish church to its right. Part of the graveyard at that time occupied the space where the 'new' main road now goes, cutting the graveyard in two; the old houses on the right have been replaced by the new fire station. A hundred yards or so further along was the cattle auction; closed down in recent years it has since seen trade of a very different kind, with hundreds of car booters congregating there every Sunday morning.

More Memories of BRADFORD II

This nostalgic view of Queensbury was taken from the top of Holy Trinity church in those long-ago days before traffic congestion became an accepted part of life. Looking north along High Street in the general direction of Clayton, a horse and cart and a couple of parked cars is the only transport apart from the two buses near the Queensbury Co-op. The familiar bend in the road towards the right has not changed, though the Co-operative buildings on the corner of Chapel Street were both demolished to be replaced by a new single-storey Co-op Food Fair and its car park.

Looking at old advertisements is always fascinating; remember 'Sleep sweeter, Bourn-vita'? The poster on the wall near the Ring o' Bells reminds us of that well-known TV jingle of the 1960s (you could probably sing it if hard pushed!), but this was obviously much earlier than that - there is not an aerial in sight in this view across the rooftops. Though it is known as the coldest place in Bradford, Queensbury nevertheless is a pleasant village and remains a popular place to live in spite of its well-deserved reputation.

More Memories of BRADFORD II

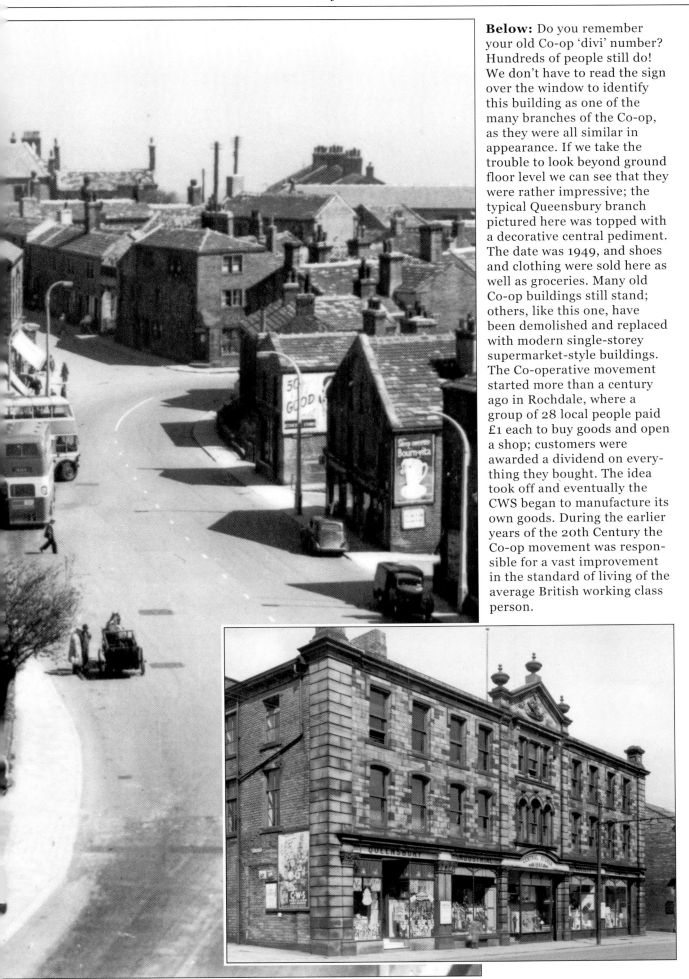

Below: Do you remember your old Co-op 'divi' number? Hundreds of people still do! We don't have to read the sign over the window to identify this building as one of the many branches of the Co-op, as they were all similar in appearance. If we take the trouble to look beyond ground floor level we can see that they were rather impressive; the typical Queensbury branch pictured here was topped with a decorative central pediment. The date was 1949, and shoes and clothing were sold here as well as groceries. Many old Co-op buildings still stand; others, like this one, have been demolished and replaced with modern single-storey supermarket-style buildings. The Co-operative movement started more than a century ago in Rochdale, where a group of 28 local people paid £1 each to buy goods and open a shop; customers were awarded a dividend on everything they bought. The idea took off and eventually the CWS began to manufacture its own goods. During the earlier years of the 20th Century the Co-op movement was responsible for a vast improvement in the standard of living of the average British working class person.

More Memories of BRADFORD II

Above: Queensbury always had - and still does have - that 'village' feel that marks it out as being much more than the average city suburb. The community is still strong, though in these days of out of town shopping centres and supermarkets, a trip to the local shops is not quite the same as it was when this photograph was taken. This section of High Street alone offered a number of shops and services, with the Halifax Building Society, Crockatts Cleaners, Carter's grocery shop and Stocks Stores. Back in the 1940s no local mother needed to think twice before leaving a child in its pram outside a shop; note the white pram and its young occupant parked outside the door of the single-storey flat-roofed shop on the right. Who would risk that today? The two Co-op buildings near the end of Chapel Street were still standing at the time of the photograph, offering local people reasonably-priced clothing and shoes as well as basic groceries. The facility that replaced it is, of course, the Food Fair, whose name tells you what kind of goods are on offer! Well-patronised, the Food Fair has become everyone's 'local shop', at least in this part of Queensbury.

Above right: The years go by, the names above the shops change, TV aerials and satellite dishes are added to rooftops, but this part of Queensbury remains basically the same. The imposing house on the left has its name, The Willows, carved in stone near the apex of the gable, together with the date, 1895; further on a road sign informs us that the Brighouse and Denholme Road crosses here. As we know, the junction grew so busy that traffic lights were later installed at this point. Morpeth Street, Russell Street and Gothic Street lead off to the right, while a pair of decorative chimney pots mark the position of the gatehouse of John Foster's Black Dyke Mills. The mill was once a main employer in Queensbury, and the cobbled yard would have resounded each day to the clattering of hundreds of pairs of clogs. Today the trade in mohair suitings, once the height of fashion in Japan, is sadly depleted and other firms now share Black Dyke Mills. Queensbury's other pride, the Black Dyke Mills Band, not only survives but goes from strength to strength. There are no trams in sight on this busy tram route; Queensbury trams ran as far as the Cenotaph, where Bradford's four-foot gauge rails met Halifax's three-foot-six gauge.

More Memories of BRADFORD II

Below: As if people didn't have enough to worry about in the 1930s Horlicks had to add to their anxiety by inventing 'night starvation'. Their adverts induced sleepless nights by reminding the hapless populace that 'Breathing alone takes twenty thousand muscular efforts every night'. Good gracious - all that breathing without food to replace the expended energy!
This fascinating array of advertisements 'somewhere in Bradford' gives us the opportunity to slip back in time to see what the sporting fixtures were and marvel at the incredible price of 6d for a packet of cigarettes. With the aid of the advert for Belle Vue Pleasure Park's centenary celebrations we can pinpoint the year to 1936, when Bradford Northern were to play Featherstone Rovers on 26th September and Huddersfield on October 3rd, while the Park Avenue match was against Blackpool on 26th September. The play 'Escape me Never' was on at the Prince's Theatre, well known to old Bradfordians. And did those Christian Scientists' free lectures entice many punters away from Thirsk Races, we wonder?

Bottom: A Number 17 trolley bus heads along Tong Street towards the Knowles Lane junction, where it will turn towards Holme Wood. This particular view has changed so much as to be almost totally unrecognisable; today, the traffic travelling towards us would just have left the enormous and very busy Rooley Lane, Sticker Lane and Wakefield Road roundabout with its dual carriageways, underpass and subways. A large Asda supermarket now occupies the area, replacing old buildings on the right, and a set of traffic lights keep the heavy flow of vehicles moving at this point. From the wide dual carriageway, Tong Street reverts to a normal-width road at around this point, which suffers from a continual flow of heavy traffic. Holme Wood estate, off to the right, was built in the 1950s to cater for the growing need for additional housing, and the trolley bus spur from the Tong Cemetery route was taken into the estate in 1960 at a cost of more than £12,500. A reversing triangle was built so that trolleys could turn at the terminus, but unfortunately it proved to be rather tricky in snow and ice. On one occasion a trolley negotiating the triangle slid ignominiously into a nearby garden!

More Memories of **BRADFORD II**

Earning a crust

Above: A scene to bring the memories flooding back to those who lived in the Lilycroft Road area during the 1940s and 50s. Corner shops were then the mainstay of day-to-day life; Jackson's off-licence shop on the right would have been a handy place for Lister's Mill workers to pick up a couple of bottles of Heys or White Rose on the way home from work! Other beverages were also on offer, however; Brook Bond tea is being advertised - and perhaps a delivery of Tizer has just been made by the lorry in the background. Was Hebden's, a couple of streets away, also an off-licence? A poster on their wall advertises Tetley's ales.

The houses seen here have changed little, and Lilycroft Road is still at the centre of a thriving local community, with many small greengrocers, grocery stores, second hand shops and self-service stores serving the residents. Smoke drifts from Lister's Mill chimney in the background, telling us that at the time this photograph was taken the mill was in its heyday as the main employer in the community.

Above right: Huffing gently like a sleeping dragon, Lister's 250ft high mill chimney is here undergoing repairs, and bristles with long ladders and frail-looking plank walkways. The intrepid steeplejacks who trusted their lives to this set-up deserved a medal for their courage! An incredible eight thousand tons of stone went into the building of the chimney, one of Bradford's most well-known landmarks - and the word 'spectacular' hardly does credit to this close-up view that shows us the true scale of the massive construction. The textile industry was Bradford's bread and butter, and when the industry declined it was feared that Lister's Manningham Mills and its fine chimney would suffer the same fate as many other mills around the city. It survived, however, and has become part of our valued industrial heritage, and though no longer leading the way in textiles the building lives on, in part at least, as residential flats.

The success of Manningham Mills was largely due to Samuel Cunliffe Lister, who together with Leeds engineer George Donisthorpe produced a machine-powered wool-combing machine. The machine could produce as much as a hundred workers, at a fraction of the cost, and Lister's rise to fame and riches (along with Bradford's woolcombing industry) was assured.

'Take a good look when it passes you!' read the adverts for the Javelin Saloon de Luxe. The de Luxe was produced at Bradford's own motor manufacturing plant, Jowett Cars Ltd, along with the Jowett Javelin, the immensely popular and successful Bradford van, and the Jupiter sports car. The impressive Javelin de Luxe could top 80mph and sold at £735 plus purchase tax, whilst its popular relative the Javelin was a snip at £635. During the 1940s and early 50s, 22,700 motors were built at the plant at Five Lane Ends in Idle. It was the Bradford van, however, that became the small firms' workhorse. Its two-cylinder nine-hp engine that made short work of the city's steep hills and its low fuel consumption made the van attractive to local companies, and twice as many Bradfords than Javelins were sold. When Jowetts ran into difficulties in the 1950s, the commercial success of the Bradford was not enough to save the firm, however. International Harvesters took over the Idle works in 1954 to manufacture agricultural tractors.

More Memories of BRADFORD II

The printing firm that's poles ahead

John Edwin Watmough, the founder of the family printing business, was a colourful character in more ways than one. Local people considered him something of a dandy, and certainly his grey bowler, spats and yellow gloves were not typical business attire in 19th century Bradford. John Edwin Watmough was born in North Street, Thackley on July 22nd 1860. His father William Watmough was one of Bradford's best known auctioneers. Ted, as he was known, attended a local private school, and grew into a young man with diverse interests; apart from his love of gay, colourful clothes - it is on record that he had a collection of some 70 ties, and that he wore a different suit every day when on his holidays, which he used to take in Blackpool, Scarborough, Torquay or the Isle of Man - his hobbies included writing and keeping rabbits. He loved animals; throughout his life he kept horses, cows, pigs, dogs and pigeons, as well as rabbits, and earned himself a reputation as a successful breeder of livestock. He was much sought-after as a judge at livestock shows, and is credited with having judged more species of livestock at shows than anyone before or since. He also became well-known as a writer in the Yorkshire dialect and was a regular contributor to Bob Stubb's Yorkshire Almanac; and this interest in writing combined serendipidously with his enthusiasm for rabbit-keeping and led, in due course, to the foundation of the family firm.

Top: *John Edwin Watmough, founder of the family printing firm.*
Above centre: *A Watmough magazine dating from January 1958.*

Ted thought there should be a regular paper with articles of interest to rabbit keepers, and in 1888 he founded one. Rabbit Keeper, as it was first called, included show reports and news items about rabbits. Ted arranged for the printing to be done by a local printer, William Byles and Son, and to bring the new paper to the attention of potential subscribers he posted hand bills in bar parlours and on Morecambe promenade. There proved to be a demand for a specialist publication of this nature, and before long the circulation had built up to the extent where it became economically viable for Ted to invest in his own printing equipment, instead of continuing to pay the mounting costs of having Rabbit Keeper printed by an outside party. Ted's first printing press was a steam-powered flat-bed press bought from Dawson, Payne and Elliott Ltd in Otley, which took 60 hours to print an issue. Soon he acquired more modern machinery which could print some 10,000 copies of a 40 page issue of Fur and Feather (as Rabbit Keeper was re-named in 1890) in an hour.

The new printing business became Ted's pet hobby, and he began to undertake printing work for a growing list of clients. Within a few years Ted was printing, in addition to Fur and Feather, show schedules and catalogues, various hand bills, posters, programmes, advertisements, magazines, Government publications, a paper for pigeon fanciers called Homing World which he himself had established, and The Shipley Express and Airedale News. The two latter he printed on green paper, just as a novelty, and he subsequently purchased The Shipley Express. Ted had installed the printing machinery in the cellar of Highgate House, his three-storey family home, and the compositors worked in the attic; as the business grew it began to take over the house, with another room becoming a reading room, yet another a manager's office, and a further two being turned into editorial offices. However, Ted's wife Kate, who was one of the daughters of William and Kate Rushworth of the Oddfellows Hall, made sure that Ted's printing activities did not upset the domestic routine; it is said that she refused to allow any printing to be done on a Monday, as Monday was washday and the cellar was required for the weekly wash. Apart from that, she was apparently quite happy to mingle family and

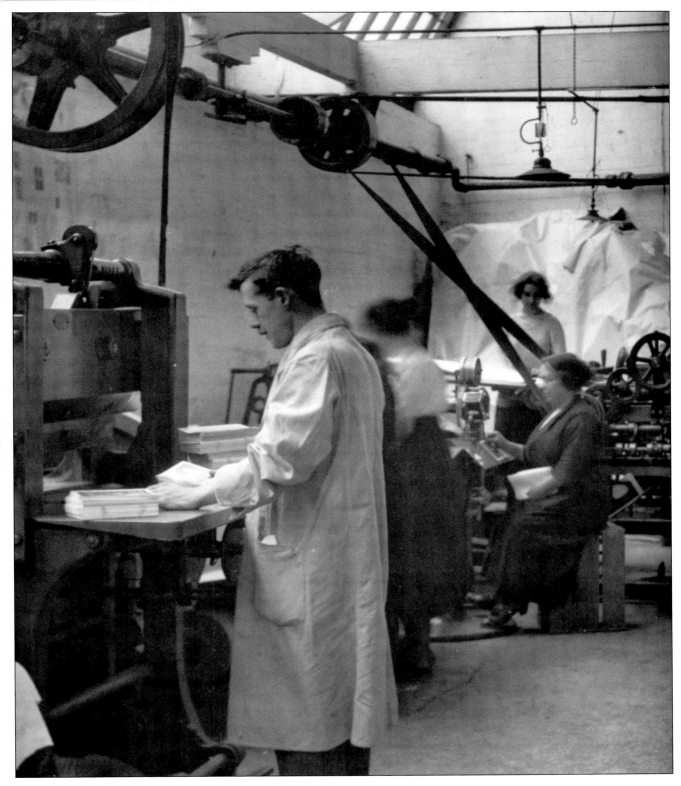

Above: *The days when a single engine drove the machines through belt driven drives and when gas provided the light.*

business duties - it is also said that she used to feed sheets into the press with one hand while caring for her son William with the other; so young William was introduced to the family business at a very early age! The family subsequently moved, taking up residence first at Plumpton Hall and later at Fairfield, and Highgate House became the works premises with the factory growing up around it.

The business which had started out as an extension of Ted's hobbies had rapidly grown into a profitable, well-established concern. In 1896 a Lino-type typesetting machine was installed, and later the same year the business was converted into a company, with a share issue to the public of 17,500 preference shares and the same number of ordinary shares. The first general meeting was held the following year, and a healthy profit was announced. During subsequent years a number of other specialist publications were acquired, including The Fanciers' Gazette and The British Canary. Profits continued to increase steadily for the next four

years or so, but in 1900 production costs began to rise and circulations began to fall, and this inevitably resulted in falling profits. In an attempt to boost business, the editorial and publishing departments of Fanciers' Gazette, Fur and Feather and Homing World were moved to 21 St Bride Street, London, in 1902; and it seemed at first as though this more centralised location had successfully restored their circulation, but the improvement proved only temporary. In 1905 the need to reduce overheads and raise capital became acute. The editors were brought back from London to Idle, and two papers, The Shipley Express and Homing World, were sold; this led to another period of profitability, but again it was short-lived. The next ploy was to divide The Fanciers' Gazette into two separate papers, Poultry World and Pigeons, but to no great effect, and profits continued to be disappointing. In 1911, the year after Ted's son Willie joined the Board, it was recognised that the fall in profits, which had at first been attributed mainly to the to the damage to the economy caused by the Boer War, might also be partly due to the fact that company's publications were failing to appeal to a sufficiently large public.

Above: *The bindery before it was moved from the main building in High Street to New Street. The picture dates from 1958.*

It was decided that a more adventurous approach was needed; strategies for recovery were decided upon, but before any significant progress could be made the carefully-laid plans were disrupted by the outbreak of the first world war. Instead, the company lost most of its workforce to the armed forces. By 1917, twenty-four of the employees were involved in the war. This was serious for a small company and the publication of Pigeons had to be suspended. Ted Watmough, who had put a considerable sum of his own money into the company - as indeed had his son Willie - took over the editing of Fur and Feather, and then made arrangements for Pigeons to be published again.

Once the war was over the company began to prosper, and by the time the downturn in the economy began to take effect it was in a sufficiently strong position to be able to ride out the depression. Again, Ted Watmough's outside interests proved invaluable to the company; Ted was a well-known figure in the world of livestock shows, and the firm was called upon to carry out a great deal of printing for livestock shows. A period of expansion ensued: in 1921 the company, which was now known as Watmoughs Limited, purchased John Hartley's Clock Almanac, followed by Dog World and Dog World Annual in 1928; in 1927 offices were again opened in London, at 10 Great New Street, EC4; and there were sufficient funds to invest in new machinery and to reduce the price of Fur and Feather. Difficult trading conditions returned, however, during the early 1930s; in 1932 it was decided that as an economy measure the annual staff outing would not take place, nor would the firm make any contribution to the annual dinner dance; and in 1933 the firm's Morris car and van were replaced by a Morris Ten and a Jowett van, again with a view to effecting economies; but 1934 saw some relaxation of these harsh measures of austerity when the firm conceded that 'the development of the social spirit among the staff by means of the annual dance and summer excursions was beneficial to the company'. Five years later the war brought a return to austerity with salary cuts and a 50 per cent reduction in the staff's Christmas presents. This was also the year in which the company sadly lost its founder: on January 6th, 1939, Ted Watmough died at the age of 78.

The second world war brought in HMSO printing contracts. There was also a tremendous demand for Fur and Feather as many families resorted to breeding rabbits and keeping a few chickens in their back gardens, for nutritional purposes; however, the company experienced some difficulties in obtaining newsprint. Fortunately Fur and Feather was classified as an industrial, rather than a specialist, periodical, and negotiations with the Paper Controller resulted in sufficient newsprint supplies to maintain production, although advertisement space was cut. Paper shortage continued to be a problem for many years after the end of the war, and indeed this was to be compounded in 1947 by the fuel crisis which restricted the use of machinery.

As soon as the war ended, the company invested in new equipment, ordering amongst other things a new rotary press which had been badly needed for some time. More space was also needed; building extensions had been planned, but the first application to build was refused by the Ministry of Works and Buildings.

Meanwhile, orders continued to flow in from the Crown Agents, and also from the local authority

Left: *Making up one of the weeklies on the stone, a steel topped table on which the solid lines from the linotypes were assembled into pages.*
Below: *The office block in March 1964. Here, in the house where John Edwin Watmough lived, the business was established.*

More Memories of BRADFORD II

who contracted Watmoughs to print the new voters' list. In 1945 Albion Mills was purchased and refurbishment including electrical wiring undertaken, and production began there the following year. The war-time ban on new publications had by this time been lifted, and, having considered fishing and field sports as possible topics, the company launched a new periodical entitled Field Sports, with the first issue appearing on January 18th, 1946. The following year brought expansion in a new direction when Alfred Thornton Limited became a subsidiary of Watmoughs; Alfred Thornton was the most advanced makers of pattern card and shade card in the country, not only making the cases and folders in which manufacturers of items such as knitting wool, cotton, ladies' stockings, tapes, curtains and floor coverings display samples of their goods, but also preparing the samples and fixing them into the cases - for example, laying ends of sewing cotton side by side and sticking them onto gummed board, or wrapping fine silks around board strips.

The family connection with the business was maintained when Willie's son, Jack was appointed a director of the company in April 1953. Later that year Watmoughs was established as a holding company, Watmoughs (Holdings) Limited, with Jack being appointed managing director in August 1954. During the 1950s the company's central concern remained the maintenance of circulation figures for its various publications, and the acquisition of new equipment. A separate small company, Highdale Limited, was set up in Idle to handle small orders. The management also continued to organise social events and provided improved facilities for employees; the Joint Works Committee was formed in 1957, with representatives from each department (except the office staff, who were not immediately forthcoming with a representative), and the early activities of this committee included the establishment of the newsletter 'Watmough News', as well as putting forward suggestions on matters as diverse as draught prevention, hot water supplies, 'flu prevention, provision of a cycle rack, apprentice training and cloak room arrangements. As growth continued, a succession of building extensions were carried out, and in 1962 mill premises in New Street, Idle were bought to house the binding department and warehouse. By 1965 some 500 staff were employed, as compared to 200, five years earlier. The Company continued to print the Empire Stores Catalogue, which had grown to become its largest single contract at that time. Watmoughs became a public company in December 1965 when Singer and Friedlander placed 420,000 five-shilling ordinary shares at ten shillings each, which raised £200,000 to finance further developments. The first-year forecast was beaten; profits were £126,924 instead of the expected £110,000.

The next 33 years brought continued growth for the Company. Patrick Walker, who joined the business in

Above: *The Board in 1963. From left to right: David Steele, Jack Watmough, Herbert Dyson, Jean Watmough, Willie Watmough, Elsie Watmough, Wally Gladders and Patrick Walker.*

1948 directly from school, spearheaded the development through this period. Businesses were acquired or developed in Hull, Scarborough, Leeds, Wakefield, Pershore, London, Budapest and Madrid. Throughout this development the registered office of the Group remained in Idle, although the Headquarters moved first into Leeds, then back into Bradford and finally to London.

The Empire Stores catalogue contract remained at the Idle plant until 1985 when the production followed the policy which had been adopted by other mail order companies and catalogue sections were printed by a number of companies in the UK and throughout Europe. Watmoughs retained some involvement, but this gradually reduced after 1985.

In 1985 the Company acquired the contract for printing the You Magazine colour supplement for The Mail on Sunday and this was produced at Idle for the next ten years. The Watmough family involvement with the business continued but finally ceased in June 1989 with the premature death of Jack Watmough.

In 1996 the Group turnover had risen to £221 million, with profits at £22.2 million.

In June 1998 Watmoughs merged with The British Printing Company, and The Polestar Group, Europe's largest independent printing company, was formed. As Polestar Watmoughs it continues to operate from both the High Street and the New Street plants in Idle, with a skilled staff of around 360 working with state-of-the-art equipment for litho planning and platemaking, web offset, binding and finishing, as well as ink jet facilities. At the High Street site, the printing department can produce up to 150,000 four-colour 32-page sections an hour. The binding and finishing department at New Street is capable of producing 88,000 stitched or bound magazines in an hour. The Company has moved a long way since the time of 'Rabbit Keeper' and currently prints and binds for many major companies: Marks & Spencer, Sainsbury's, News International, British Gas and British Telecom to name but a few. The Company also prints House & Garden and Traveller for Condé Nast and also binds Cosmopolitan, Company, Country Living and other titles for National Magazines, which are printed at an associated company in Wakefield.

In today's world of rapidly changing technology, Polestar Watmough is committed to the management of change and the realignment of working practices to ensure continuing competitiveness, while still upholding traditions of quality and service which have been an important part of the company for more than a century.

Below: *An aerial view of the company's premises at High Street and New Street, Idle.*

More Memories of BRADFORD II

Pumps for water, treacle and acid etc!

Drum Engineering was founded in the last quarter of the Victorian era, a period when the earlier discoveries of the Industrial Revolution were being improved to lighter less cumbersome designs. The company was founded by R Johnson of Bradford whose application, in August 1890, for a protective Patent on his Rotary Pump was recorded in the trade journal 'Engineering'. Patents were, and are, a legal device by which the inventor or patentee of any new or improved machine or process can claim an early monopoly on the production of their invention. Once registered patentees, who own the production copyright, may licence others, for a fee or a share of the profits, to manufacture their product.

The patent was awarded the following June for a 'drum' pump, consisting of two rotors which intermeshed like gear wheels, for use in moving liquids and air. It was quite revolutionary as, unlike existing pumps, it did not rely on valves of metal or leather fixed on rods or hinged flaps in order to move liquids.

The remarkable thing about the Johnson patented 'drum' pump is that the few working parts can be rotated in either direction. Even more valuable in variety of use is the pump's ability to move heavily viscous (sticky) fluids such as sugar syrup, molasses, unrefined crude oil, margarine and even acids. No previous pump had been able to handle such materials as even their simple working parts either became gummed together by the solidity of the substances or were unable to lift the weight of such semi-solid liquids.

These amazing machines were made, between 1892 and 1897, first in Athol Road and then in Brook Street before moving, according to advertisements in 'The Engineer', to premises in Charles Street, a story of expansion common to Victorian enterprises working in a town which was constantly changing. During the first

Top right: *28 Humboldt Street, home to Drum Engineering from the early part of the 20th Century.*
Left: *An interior view of 28 Humboldt Street.*

quarter of the 20th Century the company produced pumps for use in all conditions to be found in all quarters of the world. The range of pumps in the period catalogues illustrated machines operated by gas and the new electricity for use in the urban parts of the modern world where such refinements were available. Those in country districts may have had the use of the stationary steam engines which provided power for most factories at the time or the occasional use of a mobile steam traction engine. If these were not available there was plenty of horse power and men, to drive rotary machines, to be found up until the 1930s.

Those able to tap a plentiful supply of labour, such as the Royal Navy, tropical planters and colonial irrigation engineers, would buy pumps which were manually operated and easily transportable. The Admiralty, then and now, needs simple effective pumps which damage control parties can manhandle along narrow gangways, and occasionally up and down steep companionways, for rapid transit to the scene of fire. Marine pumps of this nature have a manual pump arm to replace the motor in case of failure.

At home Drum pumps find employment in industries such as paper mills where semi-liquid pulp from wood, straw and recycled paper is constantly being circulated. The vast and diverse chemical industry, which is so important to every aspect of our daily existence, could not operate without Drum pumps to maintain the automated flow of raw materials and partly processed substances throughout its plants. Brewers, sugar refiners, paint manufacturers and others all rely on simple effective Drum pumps to keep their products on the move.

Margarine and soap at some stages during their manufacture from amazingly similar materials may include, dependant on individual recipes, whale, vegetable or peanut oils. The Drum pumps force the pliable semi-solids along pipe lines much as we squeeze tooth paste from its tube.

Top left: *An early advert for Drum Engineering.*
Above: *A 'B.R.B.' pump produced in the late 1930s and supplied to the Air Ministry for fire fighting vehicles at refuelling depots.*
Below: *One of the largest pumps produced by Drum Engineering, with a 24" inlet diameter capable of pumping 2000 gallons per minute.*

More Memories of BRADFORD II

Producers of crude oil and petro-chemicals rely on Drum pumps and once the thick, sticky black treacly stuff reaches a port it is pumped aboard tankers to be pumped out of deep holds on arrival at the refinery. Different sizes of pumps deal with material which is turned into lighter and thinner oil fuels as diesel, paraffin, petrol and aviation spirit. There is also the flow of by-products made into medicines, fibres and fabrics and plastics.

The pre-war catalogues, which were written in a form of jargon free English which laymen could understand, describe the pumps to perfection. The Drum pump combines the advantages of the large capacity low power centrifugal, or rotary pump, with those of the high powered small capacity piston, or ram, pump in giving a high powered large capacity output. This movement of parts and fluid is achieved without any slipping, back pressure or undue friction to damage the machine or to reduce its output. It is also remarkably economical in use being simple to set up and maintain regardless of the source of turning power in factory, field, ship or primitive location.

The advantages of this marvellous invention were additionally listed as being of simple construction, valveless, and having no air vessels to cause troublesome air locks. The pumps produce a high percentage of working efficiency in return for the power expended, always a good selling point. Unlike some machines the Drum pumps operate equally well at the slow speeds produced by muscle power and unlike some more sophisticated machines they not only work well in either direction but repairs can be made by replacing one or two parts only.

It is obvious that such versatile machines saw valuable service during the two world wars and other, later, conflicts where tough simple equipment would be operated by men trained in fields other than engineering. One of the most useful models to be produced by the company was the famous 'B4' pump first made in the late 1930s. The majority of RAF fire fighting tenders were equipped with the 'B4's always on standby in fuelling bays and in the ready state whenever aircraft were landing or taking off.

During the 1940s and 50s extremely large pumps of up to 10 inches (25 cms) suction inlet diameter which stood 6 feet (almost 2 metres) high and 4 feet (about 1.3 metres) wide were made for large scale rapid movement of water and other liquids. The great grandfather of all Drum pumps was a monster with a 24 inch (60 centimetres) inlet pipe which was powerful enough to pump 2,000 gallons (9,000 litres) per minute. Those who patiently operate the small bore water pumps available in

Top: One of three 500 tons/hour fuel oil pumps supplied to the Near East in the 1950s. **Right:** Some of Drum's in-house designed compressors which led to the introduction of the first oil-free compressor.

More Memories of **BRADFORD II**

caravans may well envy such an enormous outpouring of mobile liquid which this represents.

The company made attempts at diversifying its products in these post-war decades and achieved some industrial record breakers such as a machine for slicing and buttering bread which would have been invaluable to the modern sandwich shop trade. More successful was the liaison with the well known En-Tout-Cas company which led the field in the laying to order of tennis courts and entrance driveways for the well heeled private customer and municipal parks departments. The Drum easy winding net posts held many tennis nets in the right position ready for the winners to leap across at the end of 'game, set and match'. Another product which utilised the rotary pump concept was a hand operated cleaner for tennis balls, more useful to the home owners playing on grass courts and to clubs offering a recycling service of secondhand balls.

During the early 1960s Drum found that their traditional methods of producing a large range of semi-bespoke made or adapted to order goods were losing both ground and money. With 60 employees the cost per unit was higher than would be normal in a works selling ready made standard products with few variations. The Midland Bank noted the cash flow difficulties caused by long established methods and called in the Syltone Group to investigate ways in which both Drum, and the bank's money, could be saved from going down the drain. As a result of their investigation of Drum's costs, marketing and sales Syltone decided that the firm was a thoroughly worthwhile investment providing its operating practices were brought up to date. The then owner, Mr Beaver, sold his stake to the Syltone Group who have run the company ever since.

Top: *The company decided to concentrate more on the road tanker market from the mid 1960s, the Drum pump is circled.* **Above:** *Another example of one of the large industrial pumps produced by the company in the 1950s.*

More Memories of BRADFORD II

Above: The devastating result of the fire in 1968, which nearly burnt the whole factory to the ground.

The new owners changed the range of goods produced to concentrate on manufacturing the successful, and more cost effective, smaller pumps with a rapid turn-around. The principle of making in production batches, without sacrificing reputation or quality, and selling high numbers at a sensible and attractive price which gives a reasonable profit margin allowed Drum to seriously enter the growing road tanker market.

The new venture, which has proven to be a winner, has been the production and fitting of pumps for the enormous range of road tankers which ferry everything we need in little appreciated safety around the country reaching parts which railways no longer visit. Other enterprises have been the development of a range of Drum designed and built compressors which included the pioneering first oil free compressor. This was hindered by a major fire, in 1968, which nearly destroyed the entire works, the managers at the time valiantly succeeded in saving vital equipment and stopping the oil flow which threatened to burn the lot.

The company found a temporary home in Edderthorpe Street and returned twelve months later to its rebuilt factory in Edward Street. Drum's market share rose from 5% of UK sales to a dominating 75% after which the decision was made to sell the new ranges abroad following the historic lead of the early colonial sales. By 1973 Drum had a new base in Louisville in the Blue Grass state of Kentucky, USA, from which the company could reach markets in the Americas including the fast growing and prosperous Pacific Rim.

The European market was catered for by the Bradford factory supported by sales and servicing companies set up in France, the Netherlands and Italy, all countries with diverse needs for compressors and pumps.

In the late 70s following successes close to home Drum took on the challenge of selling adapted to order oil free compressors to Japan, a heavily industrialised island nation whose mountains reduce the area of cultivatable farmland. This helped Drum win

the Queen's Award to Industry for export achievement in 1980.

A restructured Syltone Group now brings additional focus to serving the overseas operations which means that the combined Research and Development Departments have studied foreign problems in order to produce workable ideas and machines suited to the needs of customers in different locations just as they did in Drum's early days.

In 1992 Drum was divided into two with Drum International in Edward Street making pumps and compressors while Drum Engineering have moved into 110,000 square feet (11,000 square metres) of new premises at Cross Lane in Tong. Here tankers are fitted with Drum pumps for loading and unloading their cargoes. Trading with clients such as Shell, Esso, ICI, Blue Circle Cement, Milk Marque, Tate & Lyle, BT, and many other blue chip companies enables Syltone, founded by Tony Clegg, to continue to be successful and profitable.

Left: Tony Clegg, founder of Syltone. *Below:* Drum International based at the Edward Street site. *Bottom:* Drum Engineering and the tanker fitting operation relocated to the newly refurbished Cross Lane site at Tong in 1993. *Inset:* An interior view of the Cross Lane site.

More Memories of BRADFORD II

Trucks and trolleys, not lorries

Over a hundred years ago trucks, like trolleys, were small devices built to carry goods and materials around factories and yards. The transport of raw materials to a factory and the despatch of manufactured products was usually by horse drawn wagons and steam railways although canal boats still played a vital part in many areas. Young lads and lasses given the task of moving goods by handcart, truck or trolley frequently excited the ire of their seniors by falling to the temptation of playing with them within the confines of the workplace. These vehicles were invariably made by H C Slingsby.

Harry Crowther Slingsby worked for the family firm of Wholesale Bottlers in Bradford, established in 1883. Five years later he was managing the company and looking into the invention of labour saving devices. For all that labour was still cheap and relatively plentiful in the late 19th Century industrial buildings from the earliest windmills had been built with a view to reducing work and unnecessary movement to the minimum. It was normal in many factories to haul the raw materials to the top floor and allow gravity to move the products downwards as processing flowed from floor to floor.

This was excellent in so far as it went but it failed to address the horizontal movement of goods and materials from place to place along the same level of often enormous floor areas. Until Slingsbys started manufacturing their trucks and trolleys this was done on locally designed and built equipment mounted on two or more small wheels or even on sled like runners. Each industry developed its own variations in style for

Top left: Harry Crowther Slingsby. **Below:** The Bath Street works in Bradford. **Bottom:** 'The Slingsby Mixed Six' - the founder and his five sons pulling various models of a popular Lifting Truck, the forerunner of the modern day Pallet Truck, 1920.

similar purposes which differed in the weight, shape and composition of the goods moved.

The ubiquitous sack trolley known to farmers, brewers, railway porters et al was found in every work place in the land including grocery shops in the days when flour, sugar and dried fruit etc was delivered in large sacks for bagging to order for each shopper.
These trolleys were simple in design, often clumsy and weighty in appearance and yet so cleverly made that heavy loads could be moved along a paved surface with relative ease.

Another popular model was the two wheeled Trek Cart, a high wheeled flat cart with low sides and a shaft ending in a handle so that one or two people could tow it along. Up until the 1960s one could find Boy Scouts hauling their camping gear along country lanes on them while Naval Barracks kept stables of the things for Jack to ferry his kit in or for moving equipment around shore establishments without burning petrol.

The same economy of use was HC Slingsby's inspiration in building the huge variety of designs for every trade. The textile mills required trucks to contain loose bulky fibres which were ferried about in capacious wicker baskets or rawhide tubs mounted on wheels. These useful all rounder vehicles were built light enough to be pushed or pulled by one person operating in confined spaces so that size was a deciding factor as were the often greasy and uneven floors.

The 'Slingsby Rolla Rocka Lift Truck' was a patented design developed in the 1920s to load and lift half a ton (1,000lbs) in only five seconds, as easily as a standard hand truck which would normally handle only 200 lbs. The 'Rolla Rocka' used the force of gravity to form part of the lifting motion, taking a significant amount of effort away from the operator. This truck was a real 'work horse' from the 1920s right up until the end of the 1960s and was superseded with the advent of the hand hydraulic Pallet Lift Truck which is in common use today. Street traders of all marques once carried their produce in or on handcarts from the once common 'Barrow Boys' to more specialist vehicles once used by postmen, bakers and others who needed to protect their wares from sun, rain, animals and thieves.

Look for the Slingsby label on the low slung pallet trolleys used in supermarkets where store room staff will be assisted by the tall wheeled ladders and other

Above: An early advertisement for the Slingsby Rolla Rocka Truck.

trolleys like those found in today's great DIY warehouses. Nursery men, outside caterers, hedge cutters and miners alike have had their specialist needs met by Slingsby products as have airlines, dockyards and virtually every industry under the sun. Some models are still man-handled while others are self propelled by small battery powered electric motors.

On the domestic scene loft ladders, tea trolleys and hotel chamber maids' trolleys are Slingsby made as are those simple, low oblong platforms with four sturdy wheels made to shift awkward half ton pianos in narrow corridors. The Slingsby castor is a vital adjunct to the job of moving things with the minimum possible output of muscle power. The late Winston Churchill, who had a Slingsby lift installed, was at first content with the hand operated model but, as a lover of progress, had it converted within a week to the electrically powered version.

Between 1893 and 1907 the company traded from the works in Bath Street, Bradford.

Expansion in the first quarter of the 20th Century was phenomenal with showrooms all over Europe and agents around the world. The Paris office opened in 1902, two years before the celebration of the 'Entente Cordiale'. Seven years later Slingsby's acquired a factory in Paris which presented a problem known to international firms today. Britons then, unlike their fellow Europeans, did not require passports with which to travel abroad let alone in their own country as was still common in several European states! The problem was to maintain control of the family business and travel by steam ship and steam railway across national borders. Only the Germans had an air service!

The present main factory was built to order, in 1907, in Preston Street where Harry Slingsby was joined by son Cecil in 1919, as a Sales Rep, following a war in which Slingsby equipment was in high demand. A year later son Victor joined the company's French connection as a

Above: *The busy Bradford Despatch Department in the early days of the 20th Century.* **Below:** *The works on Listerhills Road, Bradford.*

van boy so that he would learn to speak the language as a native! He ran the French area until he, his wife Micette and son Jimmie caught the last ship to leave St. Nazaire as the Germans took over the Unoccupied Zone of France in 1940.

Continuing the sensible practice of putting his sons through the mill before being allowed to take charge of running it Harry Slingsby appointed son Guy as a General Office Clerk in 1924 and who, after 24 years service, became Sales Director. Leo Slingsby, too, made his start in the same lowly way but died of TB a few years later. Harry Slingsby continued to travel the world while his sons worked their way up the company ladder under his capable General Manager of the day Mr Charles Thomas Clark. He posted daily reports in the days when major cities had five postal services a day so that businesses could receive lunchtime replies to their early morning letters.

In the same decade loft ladders were introduced as one of the many innovations that Harry Slingsby was developing and patenting to keep his firm ahead of competitors. As soon as the protective Patent licenses ran out these competitors, including former Slingsby employees who knew a thing or two about truck making, would copy the Slingsby models and try to undersell them. It has always been company policy to provide equal levels of service to all customers (regardless of size). The number who subsequently re-order as satisfied customers provides one main reason for long term Slingsby success.

With the changing times designs have come and gone as working practices and labour saving machines have evolved resulting in new methods and means of moving and lifting materials and goods undreamt of a century ago. Cast iron and heavy timbers have given way to tubular and sheet steel, aluminium and plastic as H C Slingsby strive to maintain their position as a front runner in the materials handling industry with the verve and enthusiasm for the up to date which is the legacy passed on by HC himself.

With all this change it is not surprising that the customer base has altered to include modern Leisure Centres, Sports Complexes and the Service Industries. This adds to the existing traditional customer base such as the Manufacturing Industry, Health Authorities, Local and Regional Government bodies, the Ministry of Defence and the Hotel and Food Service markets.

However automated factory production lines may become there is always a need for Slingsby trucks and trolleys at the beginning and end of the manufacturing processes, now Slingsby have a Website presence too.

Top: The Preston Street Works. *Above:* The Timber manufacturing facility within the Preston Street Works.

Joseph A Hey & Son Ltd Funeral Directors

It was quite unusual at the turn of the century for men to change their occupations. The Victorian world was settled and prosperous in a way that seems astonishing to people accustomed to the uncertainties of the last decade or so. According to a contemporary hymn which ran 'The rich man in his castle, the poor man at his gate.... God ordered their estate.' Men tended to follow their father's profession or trade and literally stepped into his shoes, or rather his business or job, when he died. It was a simple solution, as old as time, to the complexities of making a living. Many traditional crafts were still practised in spite of the enormous advances made by new industries and the inventions which fostered them.

Joseph Arthur Hey was one of the adventurous innovators that made the nineteenth century such a rich and expansive era in British history. In the Belle Epoque of the Gay Nineties he was working as a wool sorter responsible for grading the daily intake of unwashed wool which arrived in the family owned mill at the junction of Thornton Road and City Road. Here he sorted the wool from hill and lowland sheep from home and the Antipodes according to its quality and the end product as carpeting or fine worsteds and broadcloth or for long lasting tweeds and serges.

When free from the demands of the mill he plied for hire, with a horse drawn four wheeler cab, such as a Brougham, borrowed from his undertaker father-in-law, outside the railway stations. This part time work was so successful that he bought two cabs of his own until, encouraged by his wife, he progressed, in 1908, to running an undertakers to cater for the post-Victorian way of death, still practised in the early years of the 20th Century. This was a natural step for a man who had married into the Manningham Lane undertaking family of Turnpenny of the firm Turnpenny and Coxon.

While turn of the century Bradford was far removed from the unhealthily dangerous place it had been in the first four decades of the 19th Century death was still a common visitor to the homes of families in all stations of life. Clean water was more readily

Top left: *Mr & Mrs Joseph A Hey pictured towards the end of the 18th Century.*
Below: *The Company's first motorised fleet of cars parked outside the garage entrance of 468-470 Great Horton Road in 1925, site of today's premises (note the tramlines and cobbled street).*

available, especially in newer houses, and sewage disposal was much better organised while medical science had made considerable advances during the Queen's long reign. Child death, however, was still frequent and consumption or tuberculosis was then incurable. The great outbreaks of King Cholera were past but infections and diseases which we can cure today were out and out killers still. Social conditions being what they were those whose diet and accommodation were sub-standard died more frequently than others more fortunately placed.

Funerals were a fact of life for which many families saved with weekly payments to their local friendly societies in order to avoid the shame of having one's beloved buried in a pauper's funeral. It is from these single purpose friendly societies that today's mighty insurance companies and building societies have grown. A man like Joseph Hey was built to be an undertaker as he was a tall imposing man who added an aura of his own to the black business uniform of Victorian England of knee length frock coat and a silk top hat. His life long love of music enabled him to conduct his business with the desired regularity of organisation, dignity and sympathetic bearing which were balm to his bereaved customers. In his spare time he participated in the tuneful activities of the Little Horton Orpheous Glee Union both as a member and as president.

Top: *Herbert Hey circa 1925 standing alongside what is believed to be their first motor hearse.*
Below: *Herbert (right) and Arthur (left) Hey receiving a new fleet of Austin Princess Limousines in 1965.*

Imbued with a desire to uphold, or better, the standards of his father-in-law's company Joseph Hey, aided by his knowledgeable wife, practised his profession with all the pride of one who does a job well. His brochures declared a policy of keeping abreast of the times, and what exciting times the early decades of this our century were now that the old Queen was dead and fashions and customs were changing in the modern world!

Heys made available every possible facility to ease the suffering of those left behind by making the last journey of the deceased loved one as dignified and memorable as could be afforded.

It is these high standards which are maintained by the present family business following in the traditions adhered to by Joseph's son, Herbert, and daughters, Florence Emily (Emmie) and Sarahannah who developed the company in the second generation. It was their generation who took the revolutionary step of replacing horse drawn hearses with motor cars in the 1920s, although horses were still kept, for a time, for those who preferred the sheer magnificence of shiny black horses bedecked with sable feathers.

In 1930 a Private Service Chapel was installed next to a dignified Reception Room where mourners could meet without being stared at. Such a facility was then unique and the thoughtfulness was much appreciated by those who found a funeral gathering in the public rooms of an hotel exacerbated their ordeal to an unbearable level. The famous department store, Brown & Muffs, ran their own Funeral Director Services for the benefit of life long clients who had furnished their homes and dressed their families under their hospitable roofs. When Brown & Muffs closed its funeral department the tasteful fittings were purchased by Heys.

When Arthur Hey took over from Herbert Hey the firm was one of the largest Funeral Directors in Yorkshire. He inherited, and kept up, the family's well deserved reputation for service and the dignity so important to those left behind. In the 1950s he bought the vacant premises at 468 and 470 Great Horton Road next to the existing premises which still contained the former stables. The entire block was redeveloped to provide under one roof the in-house facilities of joiners shop, where coffins are made, a mortuary and sufficient garaging for a fleet of vehicles. The existing chapel was kept while the comfortable reception room was enlarged and the rest rooms established.

The Chapel continues to provide a peaceful sanctuary in which a memorial service may be conducted or provide a blessed place for a dignified lying in where mourners may pay their last respects to the dead. Today Heys provide quiet, dignified Rest Rooms where loved ones which have to be removed from homes or hospitals in advance of the funeral arrangements can lie undisturbed from the hustle of modern life. These simple tasteful rooms enable relatives and friends to commune with, and pray for, the dead in total privacy.

It may surprise those who equate the art of embalming with the Ancient Egyptians and their view of the after-life that this skilled craft is still practised today. Heys are proud of their staff, not least of those who, as registered members of the British Institute of Embalmers, prepare bodies for their farewell appearances prior to their last journeys.

The visit to see a loved one can bring considerable relief to a mourner who sees their relative totally relaxed and at peace.

Left: *The Private Chapel of Joseph A Hey & Son Ltd.* **Below:** *Today's Book of Remembrance.*

It is a biological fact that the skin of the deceased has lost the marks of age and pain and the viewer sees their loved one freed from all the worries or illness which may have marked their last years.

The Hey family members still involved with the company are Margaret Hey, widow of Arthur Hey, and their daughters Joan, the Company Secretary, and Kathryn. The company offers a funeral service second to none, even providing horse drawn hearses on request! Apart from the latter, and the continuing quality and dignity, the modern funeral would appear too simple to the founders, accustomed as they were to the flamboyance of their times. As costs of personal services have risen Heys have marched with the times in offering pre-paid instalment plans. As dealing with a death in the family is complicated enough by the legal and official matters Heys help to reduce the worries by offering an all-in service which can include funeral teas to replace the traditional Wake in the family home.

In an era when many family undertakers have sold out to multi-nationals there is a welcome place for the personal touch that comes from a privately run business such as Joseph A Hey and Son Ltd, member of the National Association of Funeral Directors.

Below: The Reception Room where relatives and friends meet prior to a service. *Bottom:* Today's premises, comprising a complete funeral service under one roof. The Private Chapel entrance is seen on the far right of the picture.

More Memories of BRADFORD II

The Mill Boy, the Empress and Goats of the Golden Road

Bradford, like any Victorian industrial town, has its share of stories of young lads who made good in an exciting age of expansion. Joseph Dawson started work in an Otley mill at the age of eight in the last year of the Crimean War. During the early years of his marriage he and his two brothers-in-law went in to the wool combing and sorting business based on British wool and, later, the Australian wool clip.

By 1871 he ventured into business on his own on the basis 'the greater the risk the greater the profit'. In the hedonistic years of the 'Gay Nineties' his sons Benjamin and Allon joined him soon to take over from an ailing father. Joseph Dawson retired with the intention of convalescing in sunny Australia. He broke his leisurely sea journey by a visit to his daughter in India where he discovered the hair from the Kashmiri and Mongolian goats which he was to make famous.

Below: *A delivery lorry from the early 1950s.*

Cured, and excited by the potential of his discovery, he returned to Bradford to experiment in separating the fine down from the coarse outer hairs. So successful were the Dawsons in manufacturing the new Cashmere fabric that no lady of fashion would be seen without a Cashmere shawl. These beautiful garments were often printed in the rich Paisley patterns taken from Indian hand block textile printers, of which the finest woven could be drawn through a wedding ring. Victoria, the Queen Empress of the world's largest empire, and the dazzling Eugenie, Spanish born Empress of the French Second Empire, led the fashionable world in wearing Cashmere.

The family firm went from strength to strength enjoying a virtual monopoly in separating and processing this wonderful fibre. Their Bradford Mill's workforce rose in 1909 from 50 to 200 to cope with demand and at the coming of peace in 1918 it rose again to 350 and doubled ten years later. The Depression of the 1930s all but destroyed the business

which by then was employing Joseph's two grandsons. It was saved by turning to combing the new artificial fibres produced from wood pulp and chemical by products of the coal and oil industries although Cashmere was still used.

By the outbreak of war in 1939 Dawsons had become one of the largest combers of synthetic fibres in Britain. Although the world wide conflict drastically reduced supplies of Cashmere from China and the Soviet far eastern empire the plant was employed in weaving parachute silk. In the post war years Dawsons supplied famous Scottish weavers with Cashmere and built up a huge trade with the wealthy USA.

Since then the Bradford company has joined forces with among other, Todd and Duncan, Pringle and Ballantyne forming Dawson International, a public company capable of all facets of production from the beast's back to yours. Cashmere remains a vital item for well dressed people today, the light weight, colourful and ultra warm Cashmere is as popular in Belgravia and Paris as on the world's golf links and in the best hunting shirts. The well loved classic Camel and Vicuna hair coats are equally popular with men and women who value warmth without weight in handsome garments which reflect their taste and sense of style.

The Golden Road to mysterious Samarkand, like the equally famous Silk Road, was for centuries one of the great trading routes of the land locked world of Central Asia. Along its long, arduous and, at times, dangerous tracks travelled Cashmere and other goods prized by the Romans and other discerning buyers throughout history. The minute quantities of fibre from each goat was first hand woven in high Kashmir, from whence came the name. By the 15th century 60,000 people in India alone wove Cashmere to be followed in the 1820s by a thriving Cashmere shawl weaving industry in France worth millions of francs to that predominately rural economy.

Modern Mongolians admire Ghengis Khan with the same passion with which they ride, wrestle and practice the horse borne archery with which they once conquered the world. As nomads they tend to ignore any incursion into their lives and even the few town dwellers live in the traditional felt gers (yurts or lattice framed tents). Their livelihood comes from their goats, horses and camels all of which they milk for yoghurt making. Their cash income is made from the half pound of hair plucked from each of their wide horned goats plus the hairy wisps scavenged from thorn bushes as they moult, in the spring, in preparation for summers as extreme as the upland winters.
The precious fibre, plus that collected in the same way from the shaggy two humped Bactrian camels prized as beasts of burden, is carried for weeks slung on the pack saddles of yaks, dzos (a relative), camels and horses.

Above: *Material being prepared on the gill boxes before combing into top.*

More Memories of BRADFORD II

The journey has changed little in its boy scout elements since the days of Marco Polo, tracks are still precipitous and stony while the ad hoc bridges are but precarious arrangements of logs rebuilt after every flood.

Once across the mountains and in China the much handled bales, redolent of their journey, are ferried down rivers by rafts and sampans to the historic twice yearly Fair at Kwangchow. It is here that Bradford men would enter the oriental world of the ageless caravanserai to inspect, reject or choose and then haggle like fishwives with those to whom such bargaining is a timeless and important pleasure accompanied by endless cups of bitter green tea. In addition to buying the Mongolian and Chinese supplies of Cashmere and camel hair Dawsons sent their men to markets in Afghanistan and Iran for the same fibres. Other exotic fibres bought by Dawsons included wool from the fluffy Angora rabbit, originally from Turkey, and the luxuriously fine Vicuna wool. Long ago the aloof god kings and high priests of the Incas wore wondrous Vicuna cloaks for major religious festivals in their Andean empire.

Above: *The premises in the 1970s.*
Top: *Raw material sorting.*

More Memories of BRADFORD II

On arrival the fibres are hand sorted by colour into natural shades of white, the best, light grey and brown, work requiring an eye for colour as well as well coordinated manual dexterity. They are next blended for consistency, during which process they are cleaned, in willeying machines, of sand and dirt. The blended Cashmere or Camel hair is washed and dried just like wool in scouring machines to remove grease and adhering dirt. If you have ever handled raw wool you will know how dirty it feels.

After this follows the unique Dawson process of separating the fine down from the coarse outer hairs. It is vital to achieve the maximum length combined with the minimum damage, not easy when machines are processing a variable natural product. Combing, an ancient but updated process, then separates short and long fibres for different end products. Any remaining impurities are removed at this stage which the young Joseph Dawson would have done by hand as it was then work for women and children. The long fibre goes into woollen and worsted spun yarns for weaving and knitting or in their natural shades for scarves, gloves, hats, and jumpers for all occasions.

During their journey through the modern Dawson factory all batches are subject to rigorous quality control, particularly in the cleaning and combing stages. Routine tests are made to ascertain the content of hair, scale, nep and grease as percentages of the total. Other factors vital to manufacture and to after care life with the wearer are those of fibre thickness and length and the material's ability to regain moisture. Once Dawsons are satisfied that the material won at the cost of so much effort from the ends of the earth is up to their standards the processed fibres are baled for despatch to leading yarn spinners throughout the world.

The natural progression of this long Bradford and China connection is the recent opening of the Joseph Dawson dehairing plant in Baotou, Inner Mongolia, fitted with their own Bradford built machinery and managed by a resident Bradfordian.

It is hardly surprising that a firm honoured by a visit from the Princess Royal should sell its products to the most famous firms at home and abroad including its own Pringle, Barrie and Ballantyne. Should you gasp on seeing the price tag on a Cashmere, Camel or Vicuna garment, reflect not just on the fascinating history but also on the materials' qualities including a timeless longevity that outlives many cheaper products. This is truly a cachet of style coupled with the economy of years of wear.

Above, both pictures: *The Princess Royal's visit.*

The biggest cart horse in Bingley!

In 1875 William Rhodes Atkinson, who lived in Rycroft, started in business as a joiner. On the 11th March 1880 he purchased a joinery business near Bingley Station from Thomas Bower, bringing his brother, Robert, into partnership with him.

The business ran successfully until 1887, when a spark from a passing engine, owned by the Midland Railway Company, fell into the woodyard, and the entire premises were burned down. In March 1887 Robert Atkinson purchased Milton Mills from William Bunting, and this is the site still occupied by WR & R Atkinson today. The mill chimney from the burnt out site was used at Milton Mills as a kiln. It was laid down horizontally and had railway lines running through it. Oak was cut and stacked on bogeys which were run into the chimney and the ends were closed off. Steam from the boiler was then blown into it. It was named (very aptly) 'The Cannon'.

Very much a family business, Atkinsons has passed down through four generations. William Rhodes Atkinson had two sons; Joe and Willy, and Robert Atkinson had three sons; Tom, Robert and David, and six daughters. Joe, Willy, Tom and David all went into the family business. Joe was managing director until 1949 when he and Willy were bought out. David then became managing director. Tom had one son, Bobby, who followed him into the business. David had twin sons, David and John, and David followed Bobby into the business. Bobby also had two sons, Michael and Geoff, and Geoff joined David, Bobby, and David in the family business. Today David and Geoff (great grandson of the founder) are running the almost 125 year old family firm.

William Rhodes lived in a house attached to the mill. The stables and coach house were opposite. The ground floor of the house is now part of the factory, and the upstairs is used as a stores. The coach-house was re-designed and now houses a multi-tubular steam boiler used for heating the factory.

Robert Atkinson lived across the road at Prospect House. The house is still there and one of his daughters, Isabelle, lived there until the mid 1960s.

All the family's initials were carved on the newel posts and the large open fireplaces were carved by 'Old Yoggen', the firm's woodcarver, who was given a pint of ale from the Crown Pub just up the road, to help him along with his carving.

Milton Mills consisted of two buildings separated by a narrow cobbled road. WR & R Atkinson Ltd occupied the part of the mill known as 'The Low

Shop', due to restricted headroom on the ground floor. The building was three storeys high and joiners worked, by gaslight of course, on every floor. The machines were driven by leather belts that ran on pulleys mainly on overhead shafting.

The power was provided by a steam engine, the water for which was drawn from an artesian well under the shop floor. The source of this well is thought to be somewhere up in the Dales. The engine was manned by 'Jimmy Tin Clogs' who would blow a steam whistle fixed to the outside wall, to tell the workers when to start and finish.

The present 'Main Shop' was added later by the company and some of the retired employees still refer to it as 'The new Building'.

The part of Milton Mills not required by the joinery works at that time was occupied by John Rushton Ltd and was used as a weaving mill.

In June 1927 William Herbert Horsfield and William Henry Mitchell (the bobbin makers Horsfield and

Facing page: *Robert Atkinson.*
Below: *The workforce from the early days.*

More Memories of BRADFORD II

Mitchell), leased part of Milton Mills from Atkinsons. They continued making bobbins there until the early 1960s. That part of the factory is still known as the 'Bobbin Shop' today.

Back in the days of horse drawn transport, the firm had its own stables and at one time reputedly the biggest cart horse in Bingley. Goods were delivered locally and to the railway station. The coal cart was used to fetch coal to feed the Lancashire boiler.

Until the early 1950s tree felling was routine. The logs were brought back from the surrounding areas on the horse and cart. They were then rolled down the bank from Sycamore Avenue and lifted by crane onto a big 5ft diameter circular saw to be sliced up. The timber was kiln dried using heat provided by the Lancashire boiler.

Products

In the early days there was very little that the company wasn't prepared to make. For many years they were undertakers, mainly using elm for the coffins, with oak being used for the more expensive ones. These too were delivered by horse and cart.

As well as this they made doors for the Park Lane Hotel in London, all the deckchairs for Blackpool

Above: An early catalogue for the company's line of doors.
Top: Cutting the wood with the circular saw at the turn of the century.

More Memories of BRADFORD II

Corporation, at one time all of Bradford Corporation's cupboards used in housing, fireplace surrounds, staircases, windows, shop fronts, bank furniture, gates, draining boards, lock gates for the Leeds/Liverpool Canal, and designed and made a machine with 64 circular saws to cut peat for firelighters.

During the second world war they made ammunition boxes and duck boards as well as cases for medical supplies for the frontline. At this time the company employed a large number of women.

In the late 1960s the company decided to specialise as door manufacturers and nowadays supply local authorities and builders' merchants all over the country.

For many years the company employed over 100 people, many of whom were local Bingley families who remained with Atkinsons all their adult lives.

This number has reduced over recent years due to modern machinery and techniques. The firm has had a number of long standing employees; one of whom, Mrs June Smith, worked as book-keeper and cashier for 36 years until her retirement in 1997. Another, Mr Ernest Royston was the machine shop foreman for 50 years until he retired in 1985. Others are still with the company today. Mrs Dorothy Wilson joined the company in 1962 and there are employees in their sixties who have stayed with Atkinsons since leaving school.

Many locals will remember the 'leaning chimney'. In 1989 it was reduced in height by 20 feet. The sulphur in the smoke from the Lancashire boiler had expanded the black lime mortar so much that the top had curled over until it was four and a half feet (1.4M) out of true. Another incident involved the loss of 1,000 gallons (4 Kilo-litres) of petrol from nearby Poplar Motors which had found its way into the well which supplied the works with its private water supply.

Working with timber is one of the most satisfying of all jobs made even better when working with a firm which values the skills which can only come with experience.

Above: *Mrs Dorothy Wilson, who is still with the company can be seen here third from the left in this photograph showing the company's trip to Blackpool in 1963.*
Below: *From left to right: Bobby Atkinson, Ernest Royston (who retired after 50 years), David Atkinson (MD), Geoff Atkinson and David Atkinson.*

More Memories of BRADFORD II

Britain's biggest music store

In the early decades of the 19th Century, before the formation of regular police forces, the restive populations of the growing industrial towns were watched over by troops stationed in the local barracks. A one time singer and flautist in the choir of the Square Chapel in Halifax had joined the Royal Horse Guards (The Blues) as a bandsman. He graduated to a key role, as a trumpeter, in the days when battle field commands depended on musical signals. In 1826 his wife gave birth to their son in Halifax and, some time after, he bought himself out of The Blues and settled in Huddersfield where his wife had property which included the Britannia Inn.

Their house was demolished and enlarged to include a large room used for regular concerts and operatic performances at a time when people still sang as they worked and real music was part of life. Their son Joe had learnt to play the French Horn by the time he was four and two years later played a duet with another child prodigy. The passing of the Great Reform Bill of 1832, which gave the vote for the first time to responsible workmen living in property worth £10 pa., was celebrated by a concert given by Huddersfield Old Band, conducted by Mr Wood. The six year old Joe played the triangle on this memorable occasion and was soon being tutored on the pianoforte by the organist of St Paul's Church, who also conducted Huddersfield Choral Society.

At the age of thirteen this amazing boy pipped the post over twelve adults to become organist at the High Street Methodist Church, a post he held for 13 years before becoming organist and choirmaster at St Paul's Church for another 20 years. Joe Wood was well known as a teacher of piano and of singing when, aged twenty four in 1850, he established his first shop to sell pianos and other instruments, one of three such shops in a town of 30,000! As every respectable household throughout the reign of Queen Victoria, regardless of class or income, aspired to a piano for home entertainment it was not such a hare-brained notion as it would be today.

Soon after setting up shop, where his mother attended to the customers while he gave lessons at the back, the young businessman was given the accolade of being invited to join his local Lodge of the Order of Freemasons, which later admitted the Marquis of Ripon to membership. He married Sarah who provided him with six sons and four daughters over the ensuing ten years or so at a time when the comfortably off, unlike the poor, could reasonably expect over half their children to survive childhood. During this period his brother-in-law Joshua Marshall joined the firm as a partner. He was well known as a Conductor and became the first appointed Conductor of the Huddersfield Choral Society in 1883. Another very accomplished

Above: Joe Wood, founder of what is today the biggest music store in Britain. *Below:* A concert ensemble from 1855 arranged by Joe. Pictured from left to right Miss Newbound, Mrs Sunderland, Mr Ingersol, Mr Henry Phillips and Joe Wood.

More Memories of BRADFORD II

musician apprenticed to Joe, John North, was honoured by becoming the second appointed Conductor to the Huddersfield Choral Society in around 1890.

By 1860 he started to manufacture pianos to meet public demand for the upright models which were still found in many homes in the last quarter of the 19th century. Although his early models had wooden frames and simple mechanisms they were often used by leading lights of the Victorian music scene. In the 1870s he produced the smaller ladies' model known as the piccolo piano and, in 1877, sent son William Henry to take over an established music shop at New Ivegate in Bradford. In 1882 he moved his Huddersfield shop to Beethoven House in New Street which provided greater space to show the larger Grand Pianos which a wealthier clientele was demanding.

As public tastes were changing he gave up making the cheaper upright pianos, which could be provided by piano factories. As always he was well attuned to the ever changing public tastes for new songs and pieces of music so in tune with his successful policy of keeping up to the minute he started selling the then new Edison Gramophone. The first models operated from cylindrical wax tubes, being the shape of cylinders in the popular and successful Swiss and German Musical Boxes. The flat discs were not introduced until later. Joe Wood died in 1884, aged 57 a not uncommon lifespan for the era, to be remembered as a well loved and respected employer and a pillar of the local musical and business communities.

From 1902 control of the firm reverted totally to the Wood family, initially under the direction of Joe Wood's sons Percy, Charles and Harold. Woods have reigned ever since. Disaster struck in 1905 when the Ivegate shop was destroyed by fire and Woods took up temporary home in the Mechanics Institute, which was the fore-runner of both Bradford University and BICC. Six years later the shop was more permanently housed in Sunbridge Road where Woods stayed for 60 years. In 1964 the original shop in Huddersfield was burnt out but within days was trading again in temporary premises while three years later a branch was opened in Wakefield. Woods are in Hull too - trading as Gough and Davy.

Electronic organs first became popular in Britain in the 1960s, a demand well catered for by Woods in providing the most up to date musical instruments,

Top left: *J Wood & Sons exhibition stand in Bradford in the late 1920s.* **Centre:** *An advertisement for J Wood & Sons that appeared on the back of a Hymn sheet produced to commemorate the Coronation of King Edward VII in 1902.* **Right:** *The factory staff pictured in 1880*

equipment and expert advice. The same decade saw an amazing boom in electronic organs which has continued to this day.

The public interest in Early Music and the unique instruments upon which it is played resulted in Wood's opening the Early Music Shop in 1968, which specialises in early reproduction instruments such as the magical sounding Lutes and Dulcimers and the Nakers (drums) and Rebecs. Lovers of 18th Century music can obtain elegant Clavichords which superseded the small Spinets in fashionable homes of a period when music was an accomplishment expected of all who claimed gentility.

At the other end of the social scale but no less talented were and are the folk musicians who play to appreciative audiences in pubs and open spaces on historic instruments such as the Harp, Bagpipes, Hurdy Gurdy and the Bodhran drum. These are all from the Celtic tradition found in Brittany, Ireland, Scotland and Wales where music is part of a relaxed way of life. The Celts work as hard as anyone but the philosophy that Life's for Living is in their blood stream as much as music.

Woods also stock instruments which would be at home in South America and Spain, the Alps and Eastern Europe to be played by shepherds and other semi-nomadic herdsmen. That is not all for the rich Hill Billy style of music descended from Anglo-Celtic folk music taken by British settlers to the Appalachian mountains of the Eastern Seaboard of the USA is also part of Wood's world wide stock. Woods Music Store in Manningham Lane, Bradford is considered to be the country's largest. It is housed in three stories of well lit premises dedicated to music. It is living proof that the age old love of

Top left: *The Company's Centenary outing to Whitby in 1950.* **Top right:** *An interior view of the shop in the late 1960s.* **Below:** *The shop in Sunbridge Road, Bradford in 1967.*

More Memories of BRADFORD II

making music is alive and kicking, and where better than in the North of England where all sorts of people enjoy music at all levels. A 1986 press cutting in the company archives refers to the famous Holmfirth Anthem, 'Pratty Flowers', derived in 1857 from a folk song and still sung wherever followers of the Holme Valley and Colne Valley beagles meet to raise their voices in their second century of song. Participation in music making and choral work is a lively Yorkshire tradition which has been fostered by all the Wood family from Joe Wood's father on.

The modern workshops provide facilities for repairs to all musical instruments where skilled craftsmen will tune your favourite instrument or rebuild one from scratch. Re-making a faulty piano is rather like overhauling a car as over forty different processes are involved. The cast frames are removed and all moving parts completely refurbished to the standard that they were originally made to, if not better.

handyman musician able to put together his or her choice of instrument, be it wind, string or percussion and from Recorders to Harpsichords in complexity of design.

Woods opened their first branch in London in 1998, a specialist Recorder shop and a branch of the Early Music Shop which shows that Yorkshire leads the nation in locally produced instruments of culture.

Woods do not forget the struggling young musician who cannot afford brand new equipment. The alternatives offered range from secondhand pianos which can be leased for a monthly fee, a rental/purchase scheme which allows a rented piano to be bought and of course their 40 famous DIY kits. The latter provide a comprehensive selection for the

Top: *Technicians in the piano workshop 1967.* **Above right:** *A view of the Early Music Shop.* **Right:** *The Manningham Lane store.*

A business built with true Yorkshire grit!

Bradford is Arnold Laver's second home. The business started in Sheffield in 1920 when Arnold, the son of a Sheffield builder, returned from serving as a pilot in The Royal Flying Corps. To his Father's amazement he rejected his old place in the family's joinery works and put his savings and £300 war gratuity into a piece of land on Valley Road, Heeley. In those early days he put up his own yard fence and, like any other young business of the time, persuaded customers to pay in advance so that he had money in hand to claim a cash discount for the goods he was buying to sell. As his own Sales Director he used a bicycle, while deliveries were made by hand cart until funds were available to buy a Shire horse, called Charlie, and a dray. By the end of 1921 resources allowed the purchase of a worn war surplus Fiat lorry which was soon replaced with a more reliable English Guy lorry. By 1925 there was no fear of his Father's forecast that he would fail coming true as the expanding new firm, having already leased more land from the Midland Railway Company, bought land on Bramall Lane next to Sheffield United Football Club. The large Olympic Sawmills there were up and running in 1927.

With drive and foresight Laver's not only successfully weathered The Depression but continued to expand by acquiring AV Aston and establishing an outpost in Chesterfield in 1932. Two years later he opened up in Hull, through which the region's softwoods from the Baltic area were imported.

Arnold Laver's relationship with Bradford started in 1939. Messrs James Rhodes & Co. were packing case makers and timber merchants who had been in business since 1820. They had all the usual facilities for sawmilling and machining. Just before the war they came up for sale and Arnold decided they were worth buying. It is not known whether it was bought with expansion in mind or just as a proving ground for Arnold's son Alan.

Alan Laver joined the family business around the time of the purchase of James

Above: *James Rhodes & Co's mill.* **Right:** *Milling at Wharf Street.* **Below:** *Gangs unloading Russian timber at Hull.*

Rhodes. He left the family home in Sheffield and took up digs in Bradford. He was to remain in the city that became his home until his death in 1997.

As at Chesterfield and Sheffield, Bradford's timber supplies came in by rail, so activities were extended to the LMS goods yard at Manningham. The company continued to invest in Bradford by buying an ex-RAF hangar on Stanley Road, in 1962, to provide storage for the relatively new product ranges of plywood and sheet materials.

Bradford was also the birthplace of Arnold Laver DIY. Zetland Mills, on Wharf Street had long stood empty and Alan Laver had coveted it for potential sheet material storage. On acquiring the premises it became apparent that the floors could not stand the necessary loading for sheet material storage and so an alternative use needed to be found. An employee returning from a holiday in America recounted seeing large warehouses where the public helped themselves to ironmongery, paints, doors and hardware. Alan thought that this would be an excellent use for Zetland Mills and Arnold Laver 'Cash & Carry' opened in 1968. Thus the Company became one of the first, if not the first, DIY retailers in the UK.

The Bradford part of the Arnold Laver Group continued to flourish. By the 70s the existing sawmills on Wharf Street were outgrown and the decision was taken to move the operation to Manningham Sawmills further down Canal Road. The ten acres allowed timber and sheet material storage as well as milling facilities all on the same site. Now customers could order timber or plywood or both and have it delivered on the same vehicle the next day - thus providing a level of service that has never been matched.

The Eighties brought further expansion in the Bradford area with the purchase of Beecroft & Wightman, another old established timber merchant as well as opening a builders merchants in Stanley Road and a new DIY in the old tram sheds at White Cross, Guiseley.

On its 75th anniversary in 1995 the Arnold Laver Group of Companies had businesses in Bradford, Leeds, York, Hull, Sheffield, Chesterfield, Birmingham, Kidderminster, Reading and even Skegness. The Group employed 850 staff, with many of those being sons and daughters of Arnold's first recruits.

As it heads into the new millennium Laver's is still a true Yorkshire family business where the priorities of 'putting the customer first' have not changed since the day Arnold opened for business.

Above: Cutting an order. ***Above right:*** Zetland Mill's fire in 1984. ***Below:*** Loading an order on Canal Road.

More Memories of BRADFORD II

Drummond's Freedom Suitings

James Drummond, a Northumbrian, was first connected in 1835 with the Bradford Worsted trade from which he entered into partnership in the firm Hill, Smith and Drummond. The rigours of the Hungry Forties drove thousands of country people to work in the growing mill towns. James Drummond bought out his partners soon after the expanding firm took over part of the Lister Mills at Manningham in 1849. Business was so good in the vibrantly expansive mid-Victorian era that, in 1856, he built the huge Lumb Lane Mills from which the company still trades, but with a third of the once thousand strong work force thanks to modern technology.

By 1872 the family firm became known as James Drummond and Sons, wool spinners who supplied their own and rival weaving sheds. The growing company bought raw wool not only from the North of England but from Australia, New Zealand and South Africa too. Drummond's Worsted was sold to a discerning clientele throughout the Empire, the Americas and the Continent despite competition from the growing American and European textile industries. Although one of the virtues of worsted is the longevity of a cloth made into suits which, until well into this century, were passed from father to son Drummonds also made fabrics suitable for wear in the sometimes steamy climates of the Far East.

The weather-proof red cloth of army and hunt uniforms weighs in at 38 ounces to the linear yard while tropical suitings are as light as 8 or 9 ounces per yard. In between these valuable extremes are the fabrics suitable for winter and summer wear at home. As Britons have come to work in greater numbers than before in overheated offices and live in centrally heated homes their need for insulatory clothing has declined.

Pre-war business men wore three piece suits of 22 ounces or more linear weight, a fashion which has declined progressively in the last forty years so that many now wear summer weight cloth all year round. As fewer people walk to work or travel in unheated vehicles the demand for heavy weight winter over-coats has been reduced by the use of waxed cotton coats and the Eskimo inspired Anorak first seen on the ski slopes.

Today the Drummond Group plc produces over four million metres, or 2,500 miles, of fabric a year from over £20 million worth of the newest machinery at its Lumb Lane and Milnsbridge sites. The latter mill produces the spun yarn which is then woven at Lumb Lane before returning for dying and finishing at Milnsbridge.

Top left: *James Drummond, founder of the company.* **Above:** *A souvenir brochure produced for the British Empire Exhibition in 1924.* **Left:** *The south entrance to Lumb Lane Mills.*

More Memories of BRADFORD II

While many fashion designers offer customers the limited choice which Henry Ford made famous 'Any colour you like as long as it's black' Drummonds continue the tradition of offering customers real choice by exploiting to the full the capabilities of their staff and machines in producing cloth woven from warps and wefts of skilfully selected colours.

A sign of the times is the large scale wearing of company uniforms by people in those organisations which like to project a corporate image which emulates regimental pride. Where once the styles worn by English gentlemen were worn by Anglophiles throughout the civilised world today Drummond's designers scour the world for the latest fashion ideas to sell, both at home and abroad.

Wartime servicemen could wash their unlined wool uniforms under difficult circumstances but before the days of dry cleaning all wool garments lined with silk or cotton with canvas interfacings had to be unpicked and carefully washed and dried by hand. How the mothers and maids of those rather oderiforous generations must have dreamed of washable wool which is now a reality enjoyed by all who find synthetic fibres uncomfortable.

The company laboratory facilitates the discovery and testing of both natural and synthetic materials to ensure that Drummonds lead the field in providing fabrics for people with demanding lifestyles. School and company uniforms that can be thrown into a washing machines are a boon to busy families. Technology continues to improve consumers' lifestyle with the development of fabrics and garments that stretch and regain their shape are so much more comfortable than garments made before Lycra was invented. The advertisement for Drummond's Freedom Suitings has a totally new meaning as we reach the millennium.

Above: *A general view of the Mechanics Shop in the 1920s.* **Below:** *Company motor transport in the early 1920s.*

More Memories of BRADFORD II

Loyal commitment to the needs of much valued clients

Accountants, such as Buckles, have a vital part to play in the running of the modern world. More than ever sound financial management is an essential part of everyone's life. The growth of wealth throughout all income and occupation groups is enjoyed by some as an opportunity to display their success, but for generations saving and investing for the future has been a fundamental part of British life. It was not always so, which is why those with disposable cash tended to put it into land, which was safe and productive, before taking risks with commerce, industry and foreign ventures.

Prior to the Industrial Age landowners either employed a Steward, who was often a younger son from a similar background, to keep their books, or frequently did their own accounting. The lady of the house, and later her housekeeper, also kept the accounts which provide such an insight into life in the past. As education spread beyond the limited teaching of the classics common to all great universities there grew a class of educated men able to command a living dependent on their brains.

These Men of Business, as they were known, were an invaluable adjunct to the advancement of the Industrial Revolution. Their professional expertise was vital to preparing what we now call feasibility studies in order to recruit shareholders into unknown, risky and exciting ventures. Once a mining, transport or industrial enterprise was under way the landowners, clergy and other investing laymen relied upon the joint endeavours, and honesty, of the on site managers and the men of business to secure a return on their investments.

In 1900, or thereabouts, James Buckle began practising as an Associated Accountant in Swan Arcade. He built himself such a sound reputation that in 1907 the prestigious Royal Antediluvian Order of Buffaloes Grand Lodge of England appointed him as their auditor and financial adviser. The company proudly maintains this post today having given the RAOB over ninety years of eminently satisfactory service.

Top right: *Joseph Kershaw who joined the firm in the 1920s.*
Right: *The premises at 13 Cheapside.*
Below: *Charles Buckle pictured on an outing in 1952.*

More Memories of BRADFORD II

Charles Buckle, an Incorporated Accountant following his training with Broadley and Auker of Bradford, took over the business from his father in 1915 in the second year of the Great War. Business in the Roaring Twenties was so good that he moved into larger premises in Cheapside Chambers and took on his clerk Joseph Kershaw as partner in a partnership known as Charles D Buckle & Co. Incorporated Accountants. In those days upwardly mobile professionals were expected to buy their partnerships. These would be sold on retirement to provide a lump sum for investment in a pension.

The year of the Great Depression was marked by the arrival of Sydney Farley, a Certified Accountant, as Practice Manager. This position involved obtaining business when professional men did not advertise! The growing company moved into 13 Cheapside, and survived the war years unscathed.

The New Elizabethan Age of the 1950s was marked by the death of Charles Buckle who died at a board meeting of Brown Muff's Department Store in 1956. The following year saw the firm recognised and registered as Chartered Accountants and two years later the remaining partner, Joseph Kershaw, retired. In the same year Sydney Farley's son John, who had joined the firm in 1954, acquired the practice.

The Swinging Sixties saw Buckles move to Sunbridge Road with Eric Clayton and John Farley's brother Ronnie joining the partnership, as Sydney Farley retired after 39 years as practice manager. In 1970 Michael Atkinson joined the firm, which moved to its present premises at 9 Walmer Villas in 1975, and he became a partner in 1978.

In 1990 Ronnie Farley retired in order to devote his energies to his political and commercial interests. Three years later Ian Gill became a partner, the third modern partner to join following an education at Grange Grammar School from which a significant number of Buckles' staff have emanated. The company name changed, in 1993, to 'Buckles', when they acquired the certified accountancy practice of Ronald Hellewell, who remained as a Consultant until he retired in 1998.

Despite all the changes Buckles continues its century old tradition of loyal commitment to the needs of its valued clientele.

Top left: A certificate of the RAOB GLE.
Top right: Brown, Muff & Co, with whom Charles Buckle had a long association. *Left:* Sydney G Farley.
Below: Buckles partners and consultant pictured in the late 1990s.

More Memories of BRADFORD II

From textiles to tennis courts

In 1866 one John Mansfield started a sheet metal processing company in the Church Bank and Barkerend Road area with works on the East Parade. For almost 100 years the firm provided Bradford's textile mills with various sheet metal requirements. In those days there was no plasma cutting, nor computer-controlled folding to ease the work-load, such as the Company have today. Thin sheet metal was hand cut using tin snips or by means of a foot-treadle guillotine. A hammer, dolly and hand-operated rollers completed the machinery needed in those early days.

By the 1920s Mansfields moved into larger premises at 19 North Wing, the former stable block of the historic 17th Century Paper Hall, which had come down in the world from being a gentleman's residence. The two floors provided the company with 2,200 valuable square feet of space on two floors where sheet metal could be transformed into machine guards or ventilation and extract ducts for blowing wool or removing dust. Other goods made there were steam, drying and spinning cylinders which were hand fabricated by bending the pliable sheet metal into position prior to bolting, hand-rivetting, or soldering the pieces together.

In 1932 the Mansfield family owned just the building while Bill Eastwood had taken control of the company and as owner offered, for £120, a partnership stake to Harry Pollard, a skilled sheet metal worker employed by a Bill Thornton. Eight years later Harry Pollard bought the shares from Bill Eastwood's widow and in the last year of World War Two set on his son, Gordon, as an apprentice. At the time the firm employed three skilled men supplemented by the owner-manager working part-time on the shop floor.

The last Mansfield connection with the company was broken in 1948 when Miss Mansfield, living in retirement in Morecambe, sold the building to the Pollards. Four years after that Gordon was made a full partner following completion of a successful contract in Dublin. During that decade the son took over from his father who suffered a number of strokes before he died in 1957.

In 1966 Mansfield and Pollard proudly celebrated their centenary to be

Above: *A Mansfield invoice dated 1929.* **Bottom left:** *Harry Pollard.* **Right:** *Gordon Pollard.* **Below:** *The premises at 19 North Wing pictured in 1956.*

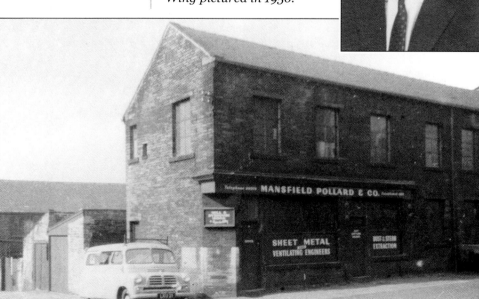

joined two years later by Barry Pollard joining as an apprentice only one year before the Company moved to larger premises in Sun Street where they employed a staff of 15. The plans for construction of the Airedale/Shipley road led to a compulsory purchase of the 4,000 square feet Sun Street works for demolition in 1971. Mansfield, Pollard moved to the former Empress Cinema in Legrams Lane where Barry, working in the drawing office, instigated a new venture in providing ventilation duct work for the construction industry.

As this proved viable, Mansfield, Pollard were increasingly less reliant on the declining textile industry. A further diversification was achieved by the acquisition in 1974 of Edwin Chambers Ltd (est 1894), makers of cowls and ventilators, and previously famous for the 'Onward' range of ovens and greenhouse heaters. Mansfield, Pollard incorporated Chambers, moving into their large Tickhill Street premises in 1978. Two years later the enlarged enterprise moved into 35,000 square feet large Crown Works in Parry Lane. The expanding company entered the field of air handling plant and ventilation canopies for large catering kitchens and food processing plants. In the same year Alan, Gordon's younger son, joined his father and brother at work. The last decade of the 20th Century had a dynamic start when Edward House, the former City and JCT Garage, was acquired to provide 45,000 square feet of covered space on a six acre site for the air handling unit section trading under the name 'Mallard', derived from the names of the two families giving the firm its title. Four years later the entire business was housed under one roof at this splendidly located and well-provided site where Mansfield, Pollard Ventilation Services, Cantech, bespoke canopy manufacturer and VAC, the acoustic and anti-vibration division, work alongside the Mallard enterprise.

The impressive client base includes projects such as Bradford Crown Courts, Morrisons at Five Lane Ends, the T & A Press Hall and the famous Alhambra Theatre. On a wider scale work has been done for Kelloggs, Zeneca and Glaxo and the leisure/tourism elements of Bass and Tetleys breweries. Other prestigious clients include Asda, the UCI Cinemas and the David Lloyd Tennis Centres.

Top left: *Staff with the Dolphin from the top of Bradford Town Hall, during its restoration by Mansfield Pollard.* **Below:** *A modern 1990s office.* **Bottom:** *The expanded company premises at the end of the 20th Century.*

More Memories of BRADFORD II

Insurance for Church and Home

The Congregational Fire Insurance Company Ltd was founded, in the likeness of many Victorian self-help concepts, by a clergyman. In 1891 Rev. S R Antliff, of Huddersfield, encouraged by the Congregational Union, set up a company to provide fire insurance for member churches. In the first nine months operating from his home premiums of £666 were received for cover on 445 churches totalling £906,000. So successful was the young company that it was not until 1904 that it actually made a loss of £337. This was counter balanced next year by a profit of £1,852 which allowed the company to continue its tradition of giving charitable grants to member church communities in need of funds for essential work under the auspices of the Congregational Church Aid and Home Missionary Society.

Following the revolutionary concept of the 1907 Workmen's Compensation Act, The Independent Insurance

More Memories of BRADFORD *II*

Company Ltd was formed to cater for expected demand and it subsequently took over the business of the Congregational Fire Insurance Company and changed its name to the Congregational Insurance Company Ltd. Two years later the decision was taken to offer private householders insurance cover which eventually, in the second half of the Twentieth Century, overtook church insurance in terms of income. Another early development was expansion into the field of engineering insurance in 1914 followed in 1919 by the transfer of the business to Apsley Crescent, Bradford.

The 1920s saw cover extended to include Third Party and Public Liability risks as the company expanded to protect churches throughout all parts of the British Isles. Following the death of the founder in 1927 the company bought the building next door for additional office space which was later enhanced by a self contained caretaker's flat. While at these premises the company broadened its remit to cover almost every class of insurance either directly or through the agency of other specialist firms.

The London sub-office was opened in 1931, and lasted 20 years, which played a considerable part in dealing with the huge burden of handling war damage insurance for HM Government. During that conflict nearly half the male staff joined the armed forces on the outbreak of hostilities. As in every other field of work they were replaced by women who grasped the opportunity of doing their bit for the country and in gaining financial independence from their families. The post war years saw an increase in the giving of charitable grants under the aegis of the Congregational Charitable Trust which now enjoys Company status.

In 1949 the company celebrated its 1941 Fiftieth Anniversary, which had been postponed due to the exigencies of war time life. The highlight of the Jubilee for the staff was a three day jaunt to London marked by official luncheon receptions and a theatrical outing with all expenses paid.

The 108 year old company today is as forward looking as it has always been in giving its customers long term relationships based upon their trust in the service provided. A revised management structure has enabled the Congregational to retain its traditional values while achieving continuous growth. Not only is the firm a registered Investor in People but money too has been well spent to create a modern office environment and investment in up-to-date technology.

As one would expect of a company established over 100 years ago to serve church communities, the firm still insures all aspects of running church buildings, including cover for the vital voluntary workers. For those in peril on the seas of the business world the company provides a flexible and competitive product based on individual assessment and rating. Home owners can benefit, as can churches, from a helpful no claims bonus system aided by a range of telephone helplines for various emergencies and legal advice. Few customers would be surprised to learn of the awards for customer service which the insurance industry has given to the Congregational.

Above: *The current Executive Directors from left to right: Paul C Taylor, Paul Moran, David J Collett and David L Goodchild.* **Facing page, top left (square picture):** *Joseph Woodhead, Chairman of the company from 1891 - 1908.* **Facing page, top left (oval picture):** *Rev. SR Antliff.* **Facing page, top right:** *Transfer of Shares Certificate from 1898.* **Left:** *Directors and staff at the Diamond Jubilee dinner in April 1951.*

More Memories of BRADFORD II

From buses to textiles

This is the best kind of success story, that of a 21 year old lad who came to Bradford to make his fortune. A real rags to riches serial which could have been set in the exciting expansive years of Victorian Bradford when ill-educated country folk and the, then despised, papist Irish flocked to the bursting town in search of work. This too is a migrant's tale of a similar friendless youngster handicapped with little learning but buoyed up with faith and ambition like so many who venture to a strange country to start life anew.

In post war Britain there was a desperate need, among some of the less well paid public service areas unable to match wages with booming industries, for semi-skilled staff to fill the jobs that many rejected. In answer to this call came Abdul Kader, who arrived in Bradford in 1957 with a float of £50 to keep him going while he sought work. The Northern cities then had a polyglot racial mixture of Jews and Poles who had fled the Nazis plus post war refugees from Eastern Europe and the once independent Ukraine fleeing the Communists. This heady cultural mix was capped in the late forties and early fifties by Italians who sought temporary work in the throbbing mills. By the time he arrived Christian West Indians, who had enjoyed the benefits of English style school and examination systems, were well established in various cities as public transport crews and hospital

Above: *Family and staff pose with the Lord Mayor of Bradford at the grand opening of their new superstore on the 10th August 1983.* ***Below:*** *A view of the busy interior of the store.*

More Memories of BRADFORD II

In the early 1980s weekly turnover was around £5,000 and son Saleem saw the potential of wholesaling to similar outlets serving the Asian communities throughout the North. The family then bought a 15,000 square feet disused garage which nowadays houses their superstore. This enterprise caters for an eclectic clientele ranging from those seeking bargain prices to those looking for top quality materials, both of which are supplied by Indian and Japanese producers. The former will produce a fifty yard run to order while the more industrialised Japanese would baulk at any order less than 1,000 yards.

The Kaders expansion of the eighties had been funded by the Leeds branch of the Bank of India which operates on a different system of collateral to English Banks. Today the Asian community from Britain and Europe accounts for 60% of turnover while native Britons make up the remaining 40% of the Shearbridge Road sales. The sale of textiles, garments, music and musical instruments, jewellery and Indian cooking utensils and luggage is worth some £6 million a year. It pays to start your journey on a bus.

auxiliaries. They and the Pakistani and Indian immigrants like Abdul Kader came to live in towns with a climate, not to mention the dialect, which even southerners from places like London consider extreme. The food was not a bit like mother's back home while the only Mosque in all Britain at the time was in London! The language difficulty was as real a poser as any other migrant finds in a new country where they stand out like a sore thumb, think on t'problem of being a Pom in Oz in the 1950s.

Undaunted the young Abdul Kader did what go-getters faced with problems do best. He out worked the natives in his desire to succeed, first of all as a bus conductor with responsibility for ticket sales and accounting, driver liaison and passenger safety on the doorless buses of the time. Within six years he had saved sufficient to pay the deposit on an old chip shop going for a grand. He continued to work double shifts, on his feet, on the buses while Mrs Miriam Kader put in similar hours as a dress maker in their corner drapery shop at 306 Great Horton Road.

For sixteen years the man and wife team served the Asian community in their Bradford heartland selling Lancashire cottons and muslins to Yorkshire Muslims intent on maintaining the colourful and modest dress codes decreed by their religion. As the British textile industry entered its sad decline the Kaders automatically turned to their homeland and neighbouring India for supplies of fabrics and speciality embroidered silks for the shop trading as Bombay Stores.

Above: Abdul Kader and the Lord Mayor of Bradford at the grand opening of Bombay Stores. **Below:** The Lady Mayoress learns the art of wearing a saree.

More Memories of **BRADFORD II**

Combing 'tops' for worsteds and 'noils' for woollens

Founded in 1904, Woolcombers Limited opened its purpose built combing mill at Fairweather Green in l958. Then known as the Greenside Combing Company, the plant was one of the most modern of its kind built on a new site to the west of the city. Despite its name, the new Woolcombers plant offered the full range of primary wool processes; sorting, blending, scouring, carding, gilling and packing. These processes took the wool from the raw greasy wool, as shorn from the sheep, to the white soft ribbon of smooth tangle free wool known as a top which is sold to the spinner for worsted production. As well as wool, Woolcombers also processed a whole range of speciality fibres including Cashmere, Angora, Alpaca and Vicuna. The new plant had every modern facility of the time to ease these processes and even generated its own electricity.

Woolcombers Limited and the Fairweather Green site was acquired by the Illingworth, Morris Group in the early 70s and became part of one of the world's largest wool textile groups. The plant's success continued despite the troubles of the group due to the economic pressures of the mid 70s. Perhaps the most colourful time in the history of the group, was the much publicised battle between US resident Pamela Mason, niece of the founder of Illingworth, Morris and the former wife of the actor James Mason, and the company's UK directors. This boardroom battle, which was heavily reported at the time, and at one point looked as though it might have been the end of the Illingworth, Morris Group, was finally resolved when Mrs Mason agreed to sell her shareholding. Despite these pressures the business of Woolcombers continued, including the development of a new shrink resisting process called SRW Superwash to help ensure the continued popularity of wool and the building of a new synthetic fibre conversion and dye plant.

Today, although the Bradford wool textile industry has contracted to a mere shadow of its former self, Woolcombers continues with the enthusiastic support of its owners. New investment means the plant can now offer the scouring and processing of loose wool as well as combed wool for tops, a full range of speciality treatments, including Kroy shrink resist treatment to run parallel with the SRW treatment, the most enormous presses to compact the wool for export and ever larger top sizes as demanded by the highly automated European spinners, including a 100 kilogram top which is unique to Woolcombers. With its origins at the beginning of this century, Woolcombers is firmly established and remains ready to serve the world wool markets for the next.

Top left: *An exterior view of the factory from 1958.*
Below: *Washing (or scouring) machinery.*
Bottom: *Initial sorting of the wool.*

More Memories of BRADFORD II

Educating the generations in Bradford

As long ago as 1832, the year of the Great Reform Bill which gave the vote to copyholders, the ambitious working men and women of Bradford formed the Bradford Mechanics Institute. Although five years before the commencement of the Victorian era, such a foundation exemplified the 19th century ideals of self advancement. So successful was the enterprise that within a year extension lectures were additionally held in the Primitive Methodist Chapel. By 1848 the voluntary body had formed, but not developed, its own School of Industrial Design and Art.

After thirty years in existence the Bradford Mechanics Institute employed their first paid and qualified teachers. Throughout the closing decades of the 19th Century the Mechanics Institute went from strength to strength buying land and opening new departments with full time staff for day and evening classes, some of which were subsidised by a direct tax on whisky to fund technical education.

By 1899 control of the Technical College had passed from the committee set up by its founders to the growing Bradford Corporation. Three years later the Education Act of 1902 made councils responsible for Further (ie adult) Education as well as for schools. The College continued to expand under its new owners through the Edwardian era and the inter-war years.

When Colleges of Advanced Technology were established in the late 1950s Bradford Technical College became one of the pioneers. A year later the CAT split into the Bradford Institute, now the University, and the Technical College, which was divided into a number of sites. By the end of the decade the latter had absorbed the three Senior Technical Institutes.

The 1960s saw expansion into the Westbrook Building and Joseph Nutter House. In 1970 Bolton Royd became part of the developing College whose Kent Wing was opened by the Duchess of Kent in 1971. Two years later BTC and Regional College of Art merged into Bradford College of Art and Technology which, in 1974, joined forces with Margaret MacMillan College of Education (ie teacher training) to create a body of 20,000 students and 400 staff. Later this became the BICC known today.

Top left: *An early etching of the College.* **Above:** *An invitation to the opening of the Bradford Technical School.* **Below:** *Grove Building pictured at the turn of the last century.*

More Memories of BRADFORD II

A visit to Myrtle Park in Bingley in 1928.

Acknowledgments

Graham Hall
Ledgard, Haworth
Walter Scott (Bradford) Ltd
Wood Visual Communication
John Leslie Burns
Malcolm Burns
Walter Metcalfe

Thanks are also due to:
Peggy Burns who penned the editorial text,
Margaret Wakefield and Mike Kirke for their copywriting skills